the complete guide to

Citing Government
Information Resources

the complete guide to

Citing Government
Information Resources

a manual for writers & librarians

revised edition by
Diane L. Garner, Harvard University
Diane H. Smith, Pennsylvania State University

with additional chapters by
Debora Cheney, Pennsylvania State University
Helen Sheehy, Pennsylvania State University

for the Government Documents Round Table,
American Library Association

Congressional Information Service, Inc.
Bethesda, MD

CIS Staff

Director of Communications: Jack H. Carey
Project Manager: Lin Brown
Production Manager: Courtenay Diederich
Proofreader: Jo-Ann Averill
Printing Services: Lee Mayer

A royalty from the sale of this publication goes to support the activities of the Government Documents Round Table, American Library Association.

Library of Congress Cataloging-in-Publication Data

Garner, Diane L.
    The complete guide to citing government information resources : a manual for
writers & librarians. -- Rev. ed. / by Diane L. Garner, Diane H. Smith, with additional chapters
by Debora Cheney, Helen Sheehy for the Government Documents Round Table, American
Library Association.
      p.   cm.
    Rev. ed. of: The complete guide to citing government documents. c1984.
    Includes bibliographical references (p.   ) and index.
    ISBN 0-88692-254-2
    1. Government publications--Bibliography--Methodology. 2. Bibliographical
citations. I. Smith, Diane H. II. Garner, Diane L. Complete guide to citing government documents.
III. American Library Association. Government Documents Round Table. IV. Title: Citing
government information resources.
Z7164.G7G37 1993
[J9.5]
016.015—dc20
                                   93-16059
                                       CIP

This manual is a revised and expanded edition of a work originally published in 1984 as *The Complete Guide to Citing Government Documents: A Manual for Writers and Librarians*.

Printed in U.S.A.

Please inquire for information on discounts for volume purchases for classroom and other uses.

table of contents

list of illustrations

Tables

Figures

preface

This revised edition of our 1984 book titled *The Complete Guide to Citing Government Documents* is an attempt to make that title more nearly true. Two factors led us to consider bringing out a new edition. When we wrote the previous edition of this manual nearly ten years ago, we had no idea how well it would be received. We considered it a fairly modest attempt to fill a void in the literature of citation/style manuals and librarianship. We tried to bring together a large number of government document types and examples of how to cite them. But that edition lacked any reference to documents of national governments other than those of the United States. We decided early on that any subsequent edition would rectify that oversight. The new Chapter 5, written by Helen Sheehy, applies our principles of citation to major types of government publications of other countries. The second factor, the application of electronic technologies to government, introduces new complexities to bibliographic citation, and indeed, the very definition of government documents has been altered. In recognition of these changes in the form of government documents we have changed the name of this book to reflect the variety of information resources. In the new Chapter 6, Debora Cheney applies the basic principles to electronic "documents" and offers solutions to the special problems they pose.

We have prepared this manual from the perspective that a bibliographic citation has four purposes. First, it should *identify* and *differentiate* an item for a reader. Second, it should give a reader some indication of the intellectual *quality* (i.e., a major study as opposed to an information pamphlet) of the items cited. Third, it should give *credit* to the ideas of other authors, as applicable. Fourth, it should help the reader *locate* the cited item. We feel that all of these purposes have equal value, and have tried to remain true to the objectives of a citation, given the publishing and distribution practices of government entities.

In determining which elements should and should not be present in a document citation, we have used their value as a reference access point as our touchstone. If the information would not help a person locate a document or if it did not provide information about the item's format, we have not included it.

Stylistically, we have tried to conform as much as possible, given our reference perspective, to ANSI bibliographic standards. Our goal is for this manual to supplement, not replace, standard style/citation manuals (i.e., Chicago, MLA, Turabian, etc.) so that a person writing a bibliography composed of documents and other monographic and serial sources will have a consistent form. We do realize, however, that occasionally certain styles (in particular, legal citations) are required by schools or publishers. In these cases, we would encourage our readers to review and use the style that is required in that particular circumstance.

In the more general sense, we would also like to stress that content should never be sacrificed to style. We would urge our readers not to become excessively concerned with the mechanics of a citation. While we would never say that style is unimportant, we would say that the anxiety caused by the demand for *correct form* is entirely out of proportion with its worth. Furthermore, when the quest for correct form causes one to omit necessary content, the integrity of the citation is sacrificed. While punctuation, capitalization, spacing, etc. are important, they can be modified, as necessary, to ensure clarity of content.

The manual is written for three primary audiences: writers, general reference librarians, and government documents specialists. To meet the needs of each, we have discussed the function of various types of documents and the bibliographic elements necessary to them, and offered our rationale for the inclusion or omission of specific elements. We have also detailed the problems arising from the quirks of government publishing, and provide clear examples to deal with them. A glossary has been included for clarification of terms, as well as an index for quick access to particular types of citation problems.

A book, even the revision of an existing book, makes extraordinary demands on the energy, time and patience of colleagues and friends. We want to acknowledge the supportive staffs of the Pennsylvania State University Libraries and the Documents Division of the Harvard College Library. In particular we wish to thank Doris Herr and Nancy Struble, whose hard work made the electronic recreation and revision of the original text seem like an easy task. We are still grateful to our original supporters, Anne Stine and Nancy Cline, whose contributions gave us a text worth revising. Finally, we wish to acknowledge the support and input of the American Library Association's Government Documents Round Table (GODORT).

DIANE L. GARNER
DIANE H. SMITH
DEBORA L. CHENEY
February 1993   HELEN M. SHEEHY

Introduction

Purposes of a Citation

A citation can serve a number of purposes. The first is a matter of honesty: you should give credit to the people from whom you got your material. A citation can also lend authority to your work, signaling your reader that a great deal of careful research went into your final product. The last, and perhaps most important, function of a citation is to provide a kind of road map for research. This is the function with which most libraries, and this manual, are primarily concerned.

A good citation should give your readers enough accurate and pertinent bibliographic information so they can locate what you have cited. The information required will depend partly on the work cited and partly on the methods of access used by libraries. The problem is that library methods are not absolutely uniform. The best you can do in creating a citation is to provide enough information to accommodate most known situations. The usual elements of a citation—author, title, place, publisher, date—while adequate in most libraries for most books, are not adequate for government documents.

What Are Government Documents?

Government documents have never been easy to define. Furthermore, the rise of electronic formats as media of dissemination has contributed to a blurring of the definition of a government publication and prompted many to speak of government "information" rather than government documents. In this manual when we refer to government documents or government information we mean information in any format produced by or for a governmental body and made public. Government information may be a pamphlet on how to quit smoking; a transcript of a Congressional hearing; an expert's report on the food needs of a developing country; a floppy disk edition of a civil service test; a magnetic tape containing census data; debates of a parliament in print, on CD-ROM, or on-line; in short any part of the activities of a governmental body that the government chooses to record and make available in any format.

Why do government documents present special citation problems? There are many reasons, but basically they all come down to this: governments do not always follow standard publishing practices, and libraries do not always treat documents as they treat books.

Government Publishing Practices

In the case of commercial publications, certain publishing practices are well established. You typically can expect to find a page with an obvious title, author, place of publication, and publisher. On the back of that page you can find a copyright date. Governments, however, do not necessarily follow these rules.

In the first place, many government documents are not meant for publication in the usual sense. Although the government may make every effort to ensure wide distribution, the majority of government documents result from the government's business and not from a desire to publish something. Thus, the publication style is developed independently by each agency with a view to its own needs rather than to a uniform style.

Second, many government documents lack, in part or in full, the elements considered necessary for a good citation, (i.e., author, title, and imprint). Many documents have only anonymous authors. Title is the one bibliographic element most likely to be found (though not always), but even title can be a problem. For example, the design of a document may present you with several choices as to title, or the title may be so long and rambling that it is useless. The imprint—place and publisher especially—is the element most likely to be missing altogether. If you follow the usual citation style and simply omit what is not given on the document, you may be left with nearly useless bits of information.

Third, electronic formats have introduced new elements with which citation styles are only just beginning to cope. Electronic media, for example, are highly volatile and can be easily altered. Therefore, the time and source of information can be extremely important. There are many different formats—compact disk, video disk, floppy disk, magnetic tapes, and on-line—to name some that are available now. Because a publication may not be exactly the same in every format, it is vital that the medium be described. These are not just issues for government electronic information, but for all electronic media. Given the volume of government information now being produced in electronic formats, finding a useful citation style for these "documents" is a necessity. As electronic media continue to evolve, so will the citation elements needed to describe them. We have identified those elements as they presently exist.

Library Document Collections

If government publishing practices have made document citations difficult, libraries and those whose catalogs and indexes serve libraries have, in the past, not made them any easier. Recently more and more libraries have begun to include documents cataloging in their on-line systems, using the same level of cataloging that the library uses for books. When a library receives a book, it prepares bibliographic records, which are most typically indexed in the on-line catalogs by author, title, series, subject, and keyword. U.S. documents may also be indexed by Superintendent of Documents (SuDoc) number. This practice is relatively recent and not universal. Many libraries still keep their documents as a separate, uncataloged collection. And many libraries that catalog current documents have not retrospectively cataloged the documents they received prior to 1976, the year the U.S. Government Printing Office started cataloging U.S. documents on-line.

This situation has been relieved somewhat by the appearance of some excellent indexes and abstracts, but the fact still remains that in few places can one find a comprehensive and cumulative list of a library's government documents collection. Furthermore, even in those cases where a library has given a document a complete bibliographic record, that record is often so complicated that it is only by chance that one ever comes across it in the file.

Given this situation, government document libraries have relied on other ways of making documents accessible. For a document citation to be useful it must take into account these other ways. These include specific book catalogs, abstracts, and indexes in which bibliographic records may be found by date, by document or report numbers, by names of agencies or committees, by keywords in titles, and so on.

Mechanics of a Citation

The elements of a complete non-document citation could include any or all of the following: author, title, edition, imprint, series, and notes. A document citation has the same elements except that the issuing agency takes the place of the author. Within these categories various kinds of data should be included, depending on their relevance to a particular document (Table 1).

The sequence of these bibliographic elements and the sequence of data within these elements follow ANSI standards (with modifications). On the assumption that few bibliographies will consist of only government documents, we have kept to a form which is compatible with other traditional forms while at the same time providing slots in which to put information necessary to the retrieval of government documents.

All of the data listed in Table 1 could not possibly be used in a single citation. Therefore, there is no point in trying to determine the sequence of the data if every one were used. There is value, however, in showing the sequence in the worst cases.

A cursory look at Table 1 will show that only issuing agency, title, and notes have enough possible components to make their construction complex. Of these the title element presents the most difficulties. The order of data in the issuing agency element is fairly well established by hierarchy. The order of data in the notes element is relatively flexible; it does not make much difference what order you use as long as you use it consistently. It remains, then, to consider the sequence of data in the title element.

Table 1: Citation Elements

Issuing Agency
Political Affiliation
Agency Name
Sub-Agency Name
Number Designator of Parliamentary Body
Meeting Place of a Parliamentary Body

Title
Date of Meeting
Number of Meeting
Personal Author
Personal Author Affiliation and Location
Non-Governmental Corporate Author
Document Type
Document Number
Report Number
Medium Designator
Patent Title
Patentee
Patent Number
Patent Date
Number of Part
Volume/Issue Number
Pagination
Number

Edition
Edition Statement
Party Responsible for Revisions
Version Statement

Imprint
Place
 - City
 - State/Province/District
 - Country
Publisher
 - Name
 - Co-Publisher
Date
 - Date of Publication
 - Date of Copyright
 - Date of Issuance

Series
Series Title
Series Number
Multiple Series Titles

Notes
Distribution Source
Format
 - Loose-leaf
 - Mimeo
Superintendent of Documents
 Number
Catalog Numbers
Microform Collection Title and
 Accession Number
Serial Set Volume Number
Joint Issuing Agency
Joint Sponsoring Body
U.N. Sales Number
ISBN/ISSN Number
Language of Work
Translation Note
Publication Type
Map Scale
Media Size
Data Format
Number of Disks
Availability Statement
System Requirements
Software Included
System Documentation

In spite of appearances, in real citations the maximum number of parts in the title element is limited. Several data are mutually exclusive. A Congressional hearing, for example, might have a date and place, but it would not have a personal author. The diagram below shows data which might be used in a single citation and data which are mutually exclusive.

Geopolitical Designation. | Issuing Agency. | Subgroup, |
    Number Designator, | Meeting Place of Parliamentary Body. ||
      Title: | Subtitle | Volume No. |
        ⌐ Personal Author | Corporate Author, | Place ⌐
        | or
        | Corporate Author, | Place
        | or   —(Report Number(s); |
        | Hearing, | Date
        | or
        ⌊ Conference Place, | Date ⌊
      Medium). || Edition. || Place of Publication: | Publisher,
Date of Publication. || (Series). || (Notes).

The worst case we can imagine is given in Figure 1. It contains an example of nearly every element of data possible in a standard citation. However, it must be emphasized that this citation is an amalgam of several real citations plus a liberal dose of imagination. It is quite unlikely that such a document would exist in the real world.

PARTS OF THE CITATION:

Issuing Agency	Subgroup of Issuing Agency

U.S. Environmental Protection Agency. Office of Research and Development

Subgroup of Subgroup of Issuing Agency	Title

Office of Environmental Engineering. *Energy Alternatives and the Environment, 1980: Handbook*

Personal Authors	Corporate Authors	Location of Corp.

by John Jones, Herbert Phihl, and Anne Lewis of Citizens Energy Systems, Inc., Boston, Mass.

Agency Report No.	Medium	Edition	Place of Pub.

(EPA 600/3-81-032; EPA-CPUB-80-28; microfiche). Rev. ed. Washington:

Publisher	Date	Series

Government Printing Office, 1981. (Environmental Protection Technology Series;

2nd Series	Notes: SuDoc No.	Alternate Distributor

Citizens Handbook Series No. 28). EP1.23/2:600/3-81; also available NTIS PB-80 103962)

Figure 1: An Imaginary Beast: The Mythical Worst Case

A more reasonable (and real) case is the citation to a NASA technical report which appears in Figure 2.

PARTS OF THE CITATION:

Issuing Agency

U.S. National Aeronautics and Space Administration.

Title Proper

Environmental Exposure Effects on Composite Materials for Commercial Aircraft

Personal Authors

by Martin N. Gibbons and Daniel J. Hoffman of

Corporate Author   **Location of Corp.**

Advanced Structures, Boeing Commercial Airplane Co., Seattle, Wash.

Report No.   **Medium**   **Place of Pub.**   **Publisher**

(NASA-CR-3502; microfiche). Washington: Government Printing Office,

Date   **Notes: SuDoc No.**   **Alternate Distributor**

1982. (NAS1.26:3502; also available NTIS NASACR-3502).

Figure 2: Real Worst Case

A double worst case can occur when you are citing a part of a non-periodical publication, because you must give information both about the part and about the whole publication (see Fig. 3 below for two such examples).

INSERTION IN HEARING:

Corporate Author   **Title of Part**

Robins and Assoc. "Comparative Analysis of Sediment Pond Design Requirements: Interim

Page Numbers

Versus Final Federal Regulations (June 13, 1979)," pp. 89-110. In

Issuing Agency

U.S. Senate. Committee on Energy and Natural Resources.

Title   **Hearing**

Oversight - The Surface Mining Control and Reclamation Act of 1977 Hearings

Date   **Medium**   **Place of Pub.**   **Publisher**

19, 21 June 1979 (microfiche). Washington: Government Printing Office,

Date **Note: SuDoc No.**

1979. (Y4.En.2:96-44).

Figure 3: Worst Cases: Citation to a Part, continued next page

PAPER IN PROCEEDINGS:

Author of Part		Title of Part		

Moghissi, A.A. "Biological Half Life of Tritium in Humans"

Report No. of Part	Page Numbers		Issuing Agency	

(IAEA-SM-232/65), pp. 501-507. In International Atomic Energy Agency.

Title		Subtitle	Place of Meeting

Behavior of Tritium in the Environment: Proceedings of a Symposium San Francisco

Date of Meeting	Report No.	Place of Pub.	Date	Series

16-20 Oct. 1978 (STIPUB/498).   Vienna,   1979. Proceedings Series

Figure 3: Worst Cases: Citation to a Part

Simplify this problem by dividing the citation, citing first the part and then the whole as shown in the diagram below. (For a more detailed discussion, see US 7, SLR 7, I 7, F7, and E7.)

Personal Author. ‖ "Title of Part: | Subtitle of Part | (Date of Part; | Report Number of Part; | Medium of part)," | Pagination. ‖ In Issuing Agency. ‖ Title of Whole: | Subtitle | Personal Author | Corporate Author, | Place of Corporation | (Report Number of Whole; | Medium). ‖ Edition. ‖ Place of Publication: | Publisher, | Date of Publication. ‖ (Series). ‖ (Notes - SuDoc Number; | Alternate Distribution, etc.).

Needless complications can arise when you try to do too much with a single citation. It is tempting, in citing an annual title over a number of years, to include everything in one citation. This is possible only if there are no changes in issuing agency, title, publication form and type, publisher, or required notes. Few, if any, government publications meet these requirements. Remember that you must cite the publication in hand, not some generic title. Thus, for example, you would cite:

NOT

U.S. Department of the Interior. *Annual Report 1849-1962.* Washington, 1849-1963.

BUT

U.S. House. 31st Congress, 1st Session. *Report of the Secretary of the Interior, 1849* (H.Ex.Doc.5). Washington, 1849. (*Serial Set* 570).

and
"Annual Report of the Secretary of the Interior," pp. 1-117. In U.S. Department of the Interior. *Reports of the Department of the Interior, 1913.* Washington: Government Printing Office, 1914. (I1.1:1913).

and
U.S. Department of the Interior. *Annual Report of the Secretary of the Interior for the Fiscal Year Ending June 30, 1939.* Washington: Government Printing Office, 1939. (I1.1:1939).

Footnotes vs. Bibliography

All examples in the text are given in bibliographic form. There is no distinction for footnotes, since the differences between these two spring from printing styles rather than from bibliographic needs. When footnotes are printed at the bottom of a page of text, it looks better if you keep the indentations uniform and similar to the paragraph. Also, since footnotes are arranged by a number, there is no need to put an author's last name first as you do in a bibliography. With the modern practice of using end notes rather than footnotes, there is really no reason why the citation form of the two should differ. However, for the sake of those who wish to maintain a difference, Table 2 gives both forms for the three basic kinds of citations.

Table 2: Citation Forms

Citation to a Whole Work

BIBLIOGRAPHY

Issuing Agency Elements (in usual order). *Title Elements.* Edition. Place: Publisher, Date. (Series Elements). (Notes).

FOOTNOTE

Issuing Agency Elements (in usual order), *Title Elements.* Edition. (Place: Publisher, Date. (Series Elements). (Notes).) Page Numbers.

Citation to a Periodical Article

BIBLIOGRAPHY

Author of Article (name inverted). "Title of Article," *Title of Periodical* Volume:Issue (Date) Page Numbers. (Notes).

FOOTNOTE

Author (name in usual order), "Title of Article," *Title of Periodical* Volume:Issue (Date) Page Numbers. (Notes).

Table 2, continued

Citation to a Part

BIBLIOGRAPHY

Author (name inverted). "Title of Part," Page Numbers. In Issuing Agency Elements. *Title Elements.* Edition. Place: Publisher, Date. (Series Elements). (Notes).

FOOTNOTE

Author (name in usual order), "Title of Part," Page Numbers. In Issuing Agency Elements, *Title Elements.* Edition. Place: Publisher, Date. (Series Elements). (Notes).

Citing a work in a footnote or in a bibliography depends on the use being made of it. In general you would use a footnote to acknowledge and identify material (quotations, data, ideas) taken directly from another source or material that you need to substantiate your position. Usually, a footnote cites a precise part of a work. A bibliography, on the other hand, is a list of sources. It may be a list of all the sources consulted in your research, or it may be a selective list of resources, depending on your aims.

Successive Citations

The *same work* will be cited more than once only in footnotes. How you handle these successive citations will depend on whether you have a bibliography in addition to footnotes. If you have only footnotes, you should give a full citation the first time. After that, an abbreviated form is acceptable. If you have a bibliography, give the complete form in the bibliography and use the short form in the footnotes.

The author's last name, a short title, and a page reference are used in the typical abbreviated book citation. In a government document citation this translates as issuing agency, short title, and page number. (For the full form of this citation see US 2.1b.)

AID. *Kitale Maize*, p. 3.

Shorten the issuing agency's name only if you can do so without losing its identification. For example, U.S. Department of Housing and Urban Development could safely be shortened to HUD for a second footnote reference, but U.S. House. Committee on Appropriations could not be shortened to Appropriations Committee without confusion unless there were no other references to documents of an Appropriations Committee.

When abbreviating a document title, make sure that you do not take out so much information that your reader will not be able to distinguish the original source. Once you have decided on a shortened form of both issuing agency and title, be sure to use it consistently.

We do not recommend the use of Latin words and abbreviations (*ibid.*, *op. cit.* and *idem*) for successive citations, because they are too often misused and misunderstood.

In a bibliography when the same issuing agency is listed in successive citations, you may substitute an eight-space underline followed by a period for the issuing agency's name. Be sure that the agency is exactly the same in all its divisions before you use this convention!

> North Atlantic Treaty Organization. The Eurogroup. Brussels, [by 1982].
>
> _____. *Financial and Economic Data Relating to NATO Defense* (Press Release M-DPC-2(82)24). Brussels, 1982. (1983 IIS microfiche 2220-SI).

Punctuation, Capitalization, and Abbreviations

Follow the punctuation given in our examples and in Table 2. Use periods between basic citation elements. Enclose the report number and medium in parentheses within the title element. Enclose the series and notes elements in parentheses. Brackets are used to tell your reader that the information was not on the document, but was derived or deduced in some way by you. Ellipses (. . .) indicate that words were omitted from a title. Titles of whole works are either underlined or italicized; exact titles taken from parts are enclosed in quotation marks, but working titles of parts are not.

In general, we recommend that you capitalize the issuing agency and author's name, titles, subtitles, imprint, and series or collection titles. Within these elements, do not capitalize articles, prepositions (of less than 5 letters), and conjunctions. Do capitalize the first word in such elements as edition and notes. When dealing with foreign languages, follow the rules for the language of the document in hand.

In using abbreviations, choose a style and use it throughout. You may find a style in a manual, (e.g., the Chicago style manual) and follow the examples throughout; or you may (and usually must) follow a style prescribed by a publisher or institution for whom you are writing. We have used standard abbreviations for state names and months. We use traditionally accepted abbreviations for Congressional documents:

House Document	- H.Doc.
House Report	- H.Rpt.
House Executive Document	- H.Ex.Doc.
Senate Document	- S.Doc.
House Executive Report	- H.Ex.Rpt.
Senate Report	- S.Rpt.
Senate Executive Document	- S.Ex.Doc.
Senate Executive Report	- S.Ex.Rpt.

Other abbreviations are taken directly from the document in hand.

Plan Ahead

Be consistent. Look at the rules before you start out and stick to them. **Remember that the purpose of a citation is to give your reader information.** The function of a citation's mechanics is to make that information easy to read, and a consistent pattern is easier to read than a random one. We strove for consistency in our examples, and they should be used as a model for your citations.

Above all do not become excessively concerned with the mechanics of the citation. While we would not go so far as to say that form is unimportant, we would say that the anguish caused by the demand for a **correct form** is out of all proportion to its worth. Furthermore, when the quest for correct form causes one to omit necessary content, the integrity of the citation is sacrificed.

You will save yourself a lot of work if you take careful notes while you are doing your research. When using indexes, take the bibliographic information, such as issuing agency, title, publisher, and date, from the index. Then you will not have to figure out the correct information from a confusing array of candidates on the work itself. Furthermore, if you are taking the information from the standard documents indexes (see Appendix B), you can be sure that your reader will be able to find the documents you have cited.

Another source of help can be found in bibliographic forms printed in the document. These go by many names—bibliographic data sheet and cataloging in publication (CIP) are two of them. What they do is bring together the information needed for libraries' bibliographic records. In so doing they also give you the information you need for a citation. You will find these mainly in technical reports and in international documents, either in the front or the back of the document.

How To Use This Manual

The text is divided into five chapters: U.S. federal, state-local-regional, international, foreign, and electronic documents. Many of the problems encountered in these five groups are similar. However, there are always problems or types of documents unique to each group. We have tried to arrange the discussion and examples so that both the general and the particular could be covered in an orderly fashion. Most of the examples given are for real documents, but, when we could not readily find examples in our collections of cases that we knew from experience to be a problem, we did not hesitate to create plausible citations.

The U.S. chapter is the model for the others. It is the longest and most detailed because, in most U.S. libraries, federal documents represent the largest collection with the greatest use. Rather than repeat ourselves at length we refer the reader to the U.S. chapter for some of the justifications for why we do what we do. Because electronic formats present some special challenges, we have elected to present these in a separate chapter that covers all the political jurisdictions of the previous chapters.

In each chapter the citation elements are discussed and illustrated in the sequence in which they occur in a citation. Each example and its accompanying text are numbered in outline form. Within each chapter there may be some variations on the basic outline in order to accommodate particular problems.

Both the Table of Contents and the Index will lead you to the section in the manual that discusses your particular concern. The Index covers titles of well-known documents and document types (e.g., U.N. mimeos). In addition, and perhaps most important, it includes common problems (e.g., what to do with report numbers).

You will find the Index a quick way of getting to the information you need. We do recommend that you read the section(s) relating to the document you have in hand, particularly when you have no idea of how to cite it. We believe you will find our explanations useful, although in most cases the example will probably be sufficient. If not, determine which citation element in your document does not fit the pattern in the example. Then, go back to the Index or consult the Table of Contents for the location of the discussion of that element.

2

United States Government Information Resources

U.S. documents are publications either written or sponsored by the federal government. These publications cover a variety of subjects and formats. They may be as lengthy and as important as the Warren Commission Report on the assassination of John F. Kennedy, as ephemeral as a poster introducing the latest commemorative postage stamp, or as timely as recently released statistics. The form of U.S. documents may be the traditional ink on paper, microform, audiovisual, or electronic.

US 1   ISSUING AGENCY

For a U.S. document cite the issuing agency as the first element, rather than a personal author. The reasons for this are:

1) indexing until recently did not consistently use a personal author;
2) indicating the U.S. government instead of a personal author will alert your reader immediately to the fact that you are citing a government document;
3) most libraries with documents collections have them classified by government agency and can more easily and quickly locate the document if the issuing agency is apparent.

The two exceptions to the rule of citing the issuing agency as the author occur when you are citing a part of a publication or a technical report. (See US 7 and US 8.28 for a description of how to construct such author statements.)

US 1.1   Single Issuing Agency

For U.S. documents begin with " U.S.," followed by the name of the agency in hierarchical order. The object of this part of the citation is to describe the issuing agency so that anybody with a standard government reference source (such as the *U.S. Government Manual*) can identify it.

> U.S. Federal Emergency Management Agency. *Love Canal: The Social Construction of Disaster*. 1982. (FEM1.2:L94).

US 1.1a   If the agency given on the document is composed of many bureaucratic levels, how do you decide which ones to include? Usually you need use only the "umbrella" department and the lowest level agency given.

> U.S. Department of Justice. Bureau of Justice Statistics. *Correctional Population in the United States, 1989*. Washington: Government Printing Office, 1991. (J29.17:989).

US 1.1b   An agency which is well known in its own right does not need to be preceded by its departmental name.

> U.S. Forest Service. *Taraghee Lodgepole: A Pioneering Effort in Deadwood Salvage*. Washington: Government Printing Office, 1979. (A13.2:T17).

US 1.1c   When in doubt, include everything. When you include more than one level of the agency, do it in order of largest to smallest; this is usually obvious from type size and/or order of agencies on the title page.

> U.S. Environmental Protection Agency. Office of Research and Development. Office of Environmental Engineering and Technology. *Energy Alternatives and the Environment: 1979* (EPA-600/9-80-009). n.p., 1979.

US 1.2   Multiple Issuing Agencies

If the document has more than one issuing agency (Fig. 4), use the first one listed. This agency will be noted in the standard indexes as the issuing agency, and citing it will help your reader locate the document.

> U.S. Employment and Training Administration. *Environmental Protection Careers Guidebook*. Washington: 1980.

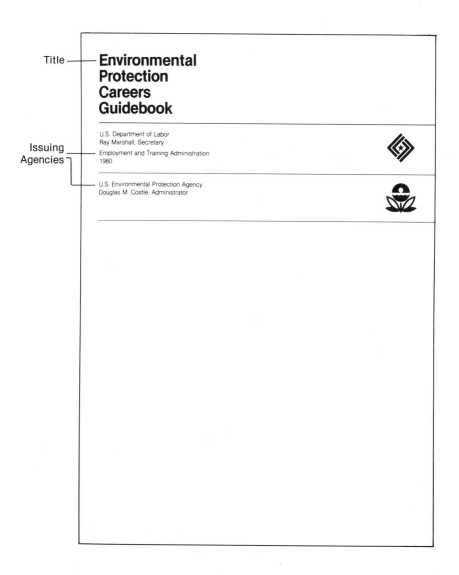

Figure 4: U.S. Document: Title Page

US 1.3 **Congress as Issuing Agency**

For Congressional publications, you do not need to include "Congress" in the hierarchical order since there is only one U.S. House or Senate.

> U.S. House. Committee on Energy and Commerce. *Seizure of Iraqi Assets.* Washington: Government Printing Office, 1991. (Y4.En2/3:102-1).

US 1.3a The one exception is when citing a Joint Congressional Committee publication. In this case you must use "U.S. Congress" and the committee's full name to alert your reader to the fact that the item is Congressional.

> U.S. Congress. Joint Economic Committee. *High Technology and Regional Development* Hearing, 1 Mar. 1982. Washington: Government Printing Office, 1982. (Y4.Ec7:T22/4).

US 1.3b If, for alphabetizing purposes, you wish to keep all Congressional publications together, you may use "U.S. Congress. House." or "U.S. Congress. Senate."

> U.S. Congress. Senate. *Year-end Report of the 2nd Session of the 97th Congress* (S.Doc.97-38). Washington: Government Printing Office, 1982. (Y1.1/3:97-38).

US 1.3c For committee prints, hearings, or reports use only the name of the main committee as the issuing agency, not that of any subcommittee. These types of documents are listed under the name of the main committee in the standard indexes and are arranged in most libraries by these committees.

COMMITTEE PRINTS

> U.S. House. Select Committee on Children, Youth, and Families. *Federal Programs Affecting Children and Their Families, 1990.* Washington: Government Printing Office, 1990. (Y4.C43/2:C43/7/990).

HEARINGS

> U.S. House. Select Committee on Children, Youth, and Families. *Babies and Briefcases: Creating a Family-*

Friendly Workplace for Fathers Hearings, 11 June 1991. Washington: Government Printing Office, 1991. (Y4.C43/2:B11/2).

REPORTS

U.S. House. Committee on the Judiciary. *Shipping Act of 1983* (H.Rpt.98-53, Pt. 2). Washington: Government Printing Office, 1983. (Y1.1/8:98-53/Pt.2).

US 1.3d With conference reports you cannot cite a single committee. Use instead the Congressional chamber issuing the report.

U.S. House. *Authorizing Appropriations for Fiscal Years 1982 and 1983 for the Department of State, the United States Information Agency, and the Board for International Broadcasting* Conference Report (H.Rpt.97-693). Washington: Government Printing Office, 1982. (Y.1.1/3:97-693).

US 1.3e For Congressional documents the issuing agency is either U.S. Senate or U.S. House, with no committee designation. These publications are in fact the product of the entire Congressional chamber, not of a committee.

U.S. House. *Columbus in the Capitol: Commemorative Quincentury Edition* (H.Doc.102-319). Washington: Government Printing Office, 1992. (Y1.1/7:102-319).

US 1.3f Acts, bills, and resolutions are numbered sequentially in the chamber in which they originate with no indication of the Congress. In order to avoid making your reader look in 102 Congresses (and 102 indexes) for a bill, you should identify the number and the session of the Congress as part of the issuing agency (Fig. 9).

ACTS

U.S. House. 101st Congress, 1st Session. *H.R. 1946, An Act To Reinstate and Validate . . . Oil and Gas Leases . . . OCS-P-0218 and OCS-P-226.* Washington: Government Printing Office, 1990. (GPO microfiche no. 393, coordinate C13).

Type of
Document

Grant/
Contract
Number

Agency
Report
Number

Title

Personal
Author

Contracting
Organization

Issuing/
Sponsoring
Agency

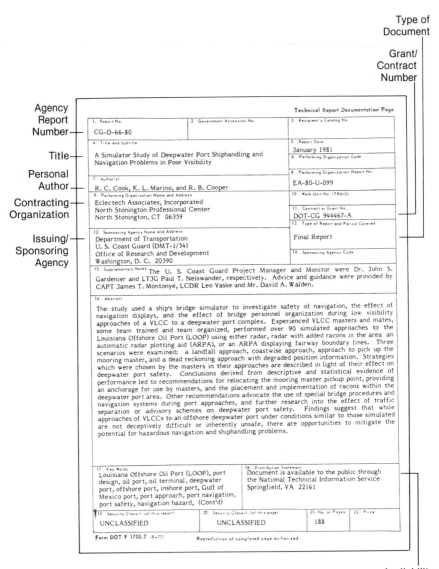

Technical Report Documentation Page		
1. Report No. CG-D-66-80	2. Government Accession No.	3. Recipient's Catalog No.
4. Title and Subtitle A Simulator Study of Deepwater Port Shiphandling and Navigation Problems in Poor Visibility		5. Report Date January 1981
		6. Performing Organization Code
7. Author(s) R. C. Cook, K. L. Marino, and R. B. Cooper		8. Performing Organization Report No. EA-80-U-099
9. Performing Organization Name and Address Eclectech Associates, Incorporated North Stonington Professional Center North Stonington, CT 06359		10. Work Unit No. (TRAIS)
		11. Contract or Grant No. DOT-CG 944467-A
		13. Type of Report and Period Covered
12. Sponsoring Agency Name and Address Department of Transportation U. S. Coast Guard (DMT-1/54) Office of Research and Development Washington, D. C. 20590		Final Report
		14. Sponsoring Agency Code
15. Supplementary Notes The U. S. Coast Guard Project Manager and Monitor were Dr. John S. Gardenier and LTJG Paul T. Neiswander, respectively. Advice and guidance were provided by CAPT James T. Montonye, LCDR Leo Vaske and Mr. David A. Walden.		

16. Abstract

The study used a ship's bridge simulator to investigate safety of navigation, the effect of navigation displays, and the effect of bridge personnel organization during low visibility approaches of a VLCC to a deepwater port complex. Experienced VLCC masters and mates, some team trained and team organized, performed over 90 simulated approaches to the Louisiana Offshore Oil Port (LOOP) using either radar, radar with added racons in the area an automatic radar plotting aid (ARPA), or an ARPA displaying fairway boundary lines. Three scenarios were examined: a landfall approach, coastwise approach, approach to pick up the mooring master, and a dead reckoning approach with degraded position information. Strategies which were chosen by the masters in their approaches are described in light of their effect on deepwater port safety. Conclusions derived from descriptive and statistical evidence of performance led to recommendations for relocating the mooring master pickup point, providing an anchorage for use by masters, and the placement and implementation of racons within the deepwater port area. Other recommendations advocate the use of special bridge procedures and navigation systems during port approaches, and further research into the effect of traffic separation or advisory schemes on deepwater port safety. Findings suggest that while approaches of VLCCs to an offshore deepwater port under conditions similar to those simulated are not deceptively difficult or inherently unsafe, there are opportunities to mitigate the potential for hazardous navigation and shiphandling problems.

17. Key Words Louisiana Offshore Oil Port (LOOP), port design, oil port, oil terminal, deepwater port, offshore port, inshore port, Gulf of Mexico port, port approach, port navigation, port safety, navigation hazard, (Cont'd)	18. Distribution Statement Document is available to the public through the National Technical Information Service Springfield, VA 22161		
19. Security Classif. (of this report) UNCLASSIFIED	20. Security Classif. (of this page) UNCLASSIFIED	21. No. of Pages 188	22. Price

Form DOT F 1700.7 (8-72) Reproduction of completed page authorized

Availability
Statement

Figure 5: Technical Report Documentation Page

BILLS

> U.S. House. 96th Congress, 1st Session. *H.R. 2, A Bill To Require Authorization for Budget Authority.* Washington: Government Printing Office, 1979. (GPO microfiche no. 1, coordinate A3).

RESOLUTIONS

> U.S. Senate. 100th Congress, 2nd Session. *S.Res. 547, Resolution . . . for a Moratorium on the Commerical Killing of Whales.* Washington: Government Printing Office, 1982. (GPO microfiche no. 24, coordinate A1).

US 2   TITLE

The title of a document, just like the title of a book, is usually obvious. However, due to graphic design and document organization, the title may be "hidden," or there may be some confusion as to what actually constitutes the title. For your reader's convenience, you should use the same title that indexes use. If you found the document by using one of the standard sources (Appendix B), use the title as given there.

US 2.1   Location of Title

If you must decide on your own what the title is, first look at the title page of the document and choose whatever title seems most prominent and provides the most revealing description of the document. Only the title proper should be underlined or italicized.

> U.S. Congress. Office of Technology Assessment. *Competing Economies: America, Europe, and the Pacific Rim.* Washington: Government Printing Office, 1991. (Y3.T22/2:2Ec7).

US 2.1a Sometimes, especially in technical literature, you will see a form entitled "Bibliographic Data Sheet" or "Technical Report Documentation Page" (Fig. 5). Since this form is intended for indexers, use the title given there.

> U.S. Coast Guard. *A Simulator Study of Deepwater Port Shiphandling and Navigation Problems in Poor*

Y4. En 2/3 · 98-18

DISAPPROVING THE FTC FUNERAL RULE
— Title

HEARING

BEFORE THE

SUBCOMMITTEE ON
COMMERCE, TRANSPORTATION, AND TOURISM

OF THE

COMMITTEE ON ENERGY AND COMMERCE
HOUSE OF REPRESENTATIVES

NINETY-EIGHTH CONGRESS

FIRST SESSION

ON

H. CON. RES. 70

A CONCURRENT RESOLUTION DISAPPROVING A RULE SUBMITTED BY
THE FEDERAL TRADE COMMISSION RELATING TO FUNERAL
INDUSTRY PRACTICES

MAY 4, 1983 — Date of Hearing

Serial No. 98–18

Printed for the use of the Committee on Energy and Commerce

U.S. GOVERNMENT PRINTING OFFICE

21-620 O   WASHINGTON : 1983

Figure 6: U.S. Congressional Hearing: Title Page

> *Visibility* by R.C. Cook, K.L. Marino, and R.B.
> Cooper (CG-D-66-80). Final Rpt. Washington:
> Government Printing Office, 1981.
> (TD5.25/2:66-80).

US 2.1b   If you are using a government document on microfiche, look
at the cover and title pages of the appropriate frames of the
microfiche. Do not rely on the microfiche header for the title,
since this information is not always accurate or complete.
You must inform your reader that the document is on microfiche, usually by including this in parentheses after the title.

> U.S. Agency for International Development. *Kitale
> Maize: The Limits of Success* (microfiche). Washing-
> ton: Government Printing Office, 1980. (S18.52:2).

US 2.1c   The title of a map can usually be found centered at its head or
in a lower corner on the face of the map. The format of the
information should be included in parentheses after the title.

> U.S. Central Intelligence Agency. *South Africa* (map).
> Washington: Government Printing Office, 1979.
> (PrEx3.10/4:So8a).

US 2.1d   If the map has no title, cite it as untitled or make up a working
title which should be placed in brackets.

> U.S. National Park Service. [Campgrounds of Yosemite]
> (map). Washington: Government Printing Office,
> 1972. (I29.2:Y8).

US 2.1e   The titles of Congressional hearings will usually be found on
the cover/title page at the head (Fig. 6). You should indicate
in the title element, without underlining, that this is a hearing;
its date (or dates); and the serial number, if any.

> U.S. House. Committee on Energy and Commerce.
> *Disapproving the FTC Funeral Rule* Hearing, 4 May
> 1983 (Serial No. 98-18). Washington: Government
> Printing Office, 1983. (Y4.En2/3:98-18).

US 2.2   Subtitles

Sometimes there is a subtitle to a document which might
distinguish a generic title or differentiate similar titles. Using

the subtitle may also help explain to your reader the relevance of this title to your research. As a general rule separate the subtitle from the main title with a colon. If the title page of the document uses some other punctuation, you may elect to use that instead.

> U.S. Executive Office of the President. Office of National Drug Control Policy. *National Drug Control Strategy: A Nation Responds to Drug Use.* Washington: Government Printing Office, 1992. (PrEx1.2:D84/992).

US 2.3 Title Length

One of the outstanding characteristics of many government documents is an excessively long title (e.g. *Abandoned Shipwreck Act of 1987; Preserving Wetlands, Historic and Prehistoric Sites in the St. Johns River Valley, Fla.; and Highway Relocation Affecting the Chickamauga and Chattanoonga National Military Park, Ga.*). You need not cite the complete title; give a sufficient portion of it so that your reader will be able to distinguish the item from similar documents and be able to locate it. To shorten a title, use ellipses (. . .) for any words omitted. You can omit any number of words provided the citation makes sense and can still be located, but never omit the initial four words of a title.

> U.S. Senate. Committee on Energy and Natural Resources. *Abandoned Shipwreck Act of 1987*: . . . *Historic and Prehistoric Sites . . . St. Johns River . . . Chattanooga National Military Park, Ga.* Washington: Government Printing Office, 1987. (Y4.En2:S.Hrg.100-434).

US 2.4 Language of Title

If a federal document you are citing is written in a language other than English, you should not translate the title, but cite it as given.

> U.S. National Institutes of Health. *En busca de buena salud fumar: este es el mejor momento para dejarlo.* Bethesda, Md.: NIH, 1982.

US 2.5   Date in Title

If the title includes a date as a part of the title, include the date, even though it may seem to be repeating the date of publication.

> U.S. Department of the Treasury. *Daily Treasury Statement, March 23, 1992*. Washington: Government Printing Office, 1992.

US 2.5a   Occasionally documents are published and distributed long after their date of origin. The imprint and title dates will alert your reader to this fact.

> *Foreign Relations of the United States: The Conferences at Washington, 1941-42, and Casablanca, 1943*. Washington: Government Printing Office, 1968.

US 2.5b   For Congressional hearings if there is a date in the title use that. Take it exactly as given and underline (or italicize) it.

> U.S. House. Committee on Foreign Affairs. *U.S. Policy Toward Iran, January 1979 Hearing, 17 Jan. 1979*. Washington: Government Printing Office, 1979. (Y4.F76/1:Ir1/979).

US 2.5c   The actual date of a hearing is not usually included in the official title (Fig. 6). It should be given in the citation after the title, but it should not be underlined (or italicized).

> U.S. House. Select Committee on Aging. *Recent Trends in Dubious and Quack Medical Devices* Hearing, 9 Apr. 1992. Washington: Government Printing Office, 1992. (Y4.Sm1:102-71).

US 2.5d   For symposia and conference proceedings give the place and date of the meeting, but do not underline or italicize them.

> U.S. Department of Energy. Technical Information Center. *Energy and Environmental Stress in Aquatic Systems* Symposium, Augusta, Ga., 2-4 Nov. 1977 (CONF-771114). Washington: DOE, 1978. (Symposium Series 48). (El.10:771114; also available NTIS CONF-771114).

US 2.6   Personal Authors

When a personal author is named in a government document, credit should be given in the citation. Place the name (or names) in normal order after the title and state the author's role (e.g., "by," "edited by"). Personal authors are those who write, compute, edit, prepare, draw, create, etc. Personal authors are not those who direct, supervise, order, or administer.

> U.S. Library of Congress. The Center for the Book. *The History of Books: A Guide to Selected Resources in the Library of Congress* by Alice D. Schreyer. Washington: Government Printing Office, 1987. (LC1.6/4:H62).

US 2.6a   If more than three authors are mentioned, name only the first and include the others in "et al." or "and others."

> U.S. Department of Education. National Center for Education Statistics. *The 1990 Science Report Card: NAEP's Assessment of Fourth, Eighth, and Twelfth Graders* by Lee R. Jones et al. Washington, 1992. (ED1.302:Sci1).

US 2.7   Contractors as Authors

Sometimes an agency will contract with a private company to produce a document (see also US 8.28a and e). In such a case, give credit to the contracting company, as though it were an individual.

> U.S. Department of Housing and Urban Development. *Rehabilitation Guidelines 1982: 10 Guidelines on the Rehabilitation of Walls, Windows, and Roofs* prepared by National Institute of Building Sciences. Washington: Government Printing Office, 1983. (HH1.6/3:R26/8/982).

US 2.8   Agency Numbering Systems

Some documents have printed on the cover and/or title page a combination of numbers and letters called "agency report numbers." These numbers should be included in the citation for several reasons:

Figure 7: Agency Report Number Example

1) they are unique to each document;
2) many libraries use these numbers as part of the call number;
3) some indexes provide access by these numbers.

These numbers frequently appear on the title page (Fig. 7). If your document provides a Bibliographic Data Sheet or Technical Report Documentation Page (Fig. 5), the report number will be provided in a box labeled "report/accession number."

Do not confuse an agency report number with the classification number added by a library (Fig. 7). Do not confuse an agency report number with a contract or grant number. Grant/contract numbers are not unique to a document, but are instead applied to every document which is a product of that contract or grant. Grant/contract numbers are usually indicated on the document by "Grant No. xxx" or "Contract No. xxx."

Agency report numbers should be placed in parentheses immediately after the title/personal author statement. These report numbers should be taken exactly as they appear on the document.

CONGRESSIONAL HEARING NUMBER

> U.S. Senate. Committee on Banking, Housing, and Urban Affairs. *Gold and Silver Coinage Proposals* Hearing, 15 Apr. 1983 (S.Hrg.98-113). Washington: Government Printing Office, 1983. (Y4.B22/3:S.Hrg.98-113).

CONGRESSIONAL REPORT NUMBER

> U.S. House. Select Committee To Investigate Covert Arms Transactions with Iran. *Report of the Congressional Committees Investigating the Iran-Contra Affair* (H.Rpt.100-133; S.Rpt.100-216). Washington: Government Printing Office, 1988.

PUBLICATION NUMBER

> U.S. National Center for Health Statistics. *Family Structure and Children's Health: United States, 1988.* (DHHS Pub. No. PHS 91-1506). Washington: Government Printing Office, 1991. (Vital and Health

> Statistics Series 10: Data from the National Health
> Survey No. 178). (HE20.6209:10/178).

REPORT NUMBER

> U.S. Energy Information Administration. *Annual Energy
> Review, 1991* (DOE/EIA-0384(91)). Washington:
> Government Printing Office, 1992. (E3.112:991).

US 2.9   **Medium**

The traditional medium of government documents has been
"ink on paper:" books, periodicals, maps, posters. New
technologies have introduced new media—microforms,
computer tapes, floppy disks, CD-ROMs, slides, motion
pictures, and audio or video tapes. The reasons for indicating
the medium in a bibliographic citation are:

1) media other than books and periodicals may require special
   housing and may be placed in separate locations in libraries;
2) media other than ink on paper may require special equipment
   for use;
3) media other than ink on paper may be indexed only in special
   resources.

You should name the medium for audio or video tapes, audiovisual material, computer tapes, film strips, maps, microforms, and slides. Medium goes in parentheses after the title,
personal author, and report number.

CASSETTE

> U.S. Department of Labor. Women's Bureau. *Legal
> Rights of Women Workers* (audio cassette). Washing-
> ton, 1976.

COMPUTER FILE, TAPE, OR DATA (see Chapter 6)

MAP

> U.S. Central Intelligence Agency. *Major Shipping
> Routes of the World* (map). Washington: Government
> Printing Office, 1978.

MICROFICHE

> U.S. Bureau of Outdoor Recreation. *National Urban
> Recreation Study: Dallas Fort Worth* (microfiche).

Washington: Government Printing Office, 1977. (I66.24:D16).

US 2.9a You need not indicate the medium when you include the information in a note (see US 6).

> U.S. Senate. *History of the Committee on Finance* (S.Doc.95-27). Washington: Government Printing Office, 1977. (1977 CIS microfiche S360-1).

US 3 EDITION

Sometimes a document will be revised and published a number of times with differing content. Examples of this would be the issuance of an environmental impact statement in draft and final form, or a particular edition of the Surgeon General's report, *Smoking and Health*. Since the content may differ, you must inform your reader.

US 3.1 Edition Statement

Include the edition after the title data.

> U.S. Office of Personnel Management. *Resource Allocation Plan Model for Special Emphasis Program Managers* (OAEP-10). Ltd. ed. Washington: Government Printing Office, 1983. (PM1.2:R31).

US 3.1a If the edition is already indicated by the title, you need not repeat it.

> U.S. Bureau of Land Management. *Draft Environmental Impact Statement: Transcolorado Gas Transmission Project*. Washington: Government Printing Office, 1991. (I1.98:T68/draft).

US 3.1b If the edition is indicated in the report number, you need not repeat it.

> U.S. Department of Housing and Urban Development. *Public Housing Development Handbook* (HUD Handbook 7417.1, Rev.1). Washington: Government Printing Office, 1980. (HH1.6/6:7417.1).

US 3.2 **Map Edition**

A map can also be reissued with changes and be known as "photorevised." Be sure to indicate that to your reader if you have such an item.

> U.S. Geological Survey. *Julian, Pa.* (map). Photorevised 1987. Washington: USGS, 1962. (1:2500).

US 4 **IMPRINT**

"Imprint" is a bibliographic term for the facts of publication, including place of publication, publisher, and date. The rationale for including these data is to distinguish among titles and to alert the reader to a potential source for an item.

US 4.1 **Place of Publication**

The place of publication can usually be found on the front or the back of the title page. Sometimes it will be found on the bottom of the last page of the text. If the item is available from or printed by GPO, the place is assumed to be Washington, D.C.

> U.S. Library of Congress. *Wilbur & Orville Wright: Pictorial Materials* by Arthur G. Renstrom. Washington: Government Printing Office, 1982. (LC1.6/4:W93).

US 4.1a Should this not be the case, look for the mailing address on the back of the document, in a preface, or in a letter of transmittal.

> U.S. Forest Service. *Estimating Soil Erosion Using an Erosion Bridge* by Darlene G. Blaney and Gordon E. Warrington (WSDG-TP-00008). Fort Collins, Colo., 1983.

US 4.1b If you cannot make a reasonable guess as to the place of publication, use "n.p." (no place).

> U.S. Federal Insurance Administration. *In the Event of a Flood.* n.p., 1983.

US 4.2   Publisher

Publishing practices in the federal government are not quite the same as those in the commercial sector. Strictly speaking, agencies are the publishers since they alone have editorial control. However, citing the GPO, NTIS, or ERIC (i.e., the major printers/distributors) will lead your reader more quickly to the relevant indexes and to a source for purchase (see US 8.28). The publisher can usually be found on the front or the back of the title page or on the bottom of the last page of text. If the GPO is named anywhere on the document as printer, publisher, or sales agent, assume that it is the publisher.

US 4.2a   Sometimes the agencies themselves are the source of the document. This may be indicated on a mailing label, in a letter of transmittal in the document itself, or on a bibliographic data sheet. In such cases, the agency can be assumed to be the publisher. If the name has already been given in full as the author, you may abbreviate.

> U.S. National Defense University. *Afghanistan: The First Five Years of Soviet Occupation* by Bruce Armstutz. Washington: NDU Press, 1986. (D5.402:Af3).

US 4.2b   If you cannot determine a publisher, simply give the place and date of publication.

> U.S. Forest Service. *Estimating Soil Erosion Using an Erosion Bridge* by Darlene G. Blaney and Gordon E. Warrington (WSDG-TP-0008). Fort Collins, Colo., 1983.

US 4.3   Date of Publication

The date of publication is essential for later location and verification of an item since few of the standard indexes are totally cumulative. The date of publication can be found in a number of places: title page, front or back; embedded in a report number; in a preface or a letter of transmittal; or at the bottom of the last page.

> U.S. Department of State. *Soviet Active Measures,*
> *September 1983.* Washington: Government Printing
> Office, 1983. (Special Report No. 110).
> (S1.129:110).

US 4.3a If the document has no printed date, but does have a library
date-stamp, use that date in brackets with "by." This will tell
your reader that the document would have been published by
that date.

> U.S. Department of Defense. *Radar Training Manual*
> (DATM 90-2-AX). Washington: DOD, [by 1975].

US 4.3b If you cannot find a date, use "n.d." (no date).

> U.S. Forest Service. Pacific Northwest Region. *Forests*
> *for the Future: Growing New Forests in the Pacific*
> *Northwest.* n.p., n.d. (6 leaflets).

US 5 SERIES

A series is a group of publications under one group title with
distinct titles for individual works. Individual titles may or
may not be numbered. It is a good idea to include series in a
citation because:

1) it is often a shortcut in locating the document;
2) if a bibliographic record (index, catalog, etc.) does not
   distinguish individual titles in series, the series name may be
   the *only* way of locating it.

US 5.1 Series Name and Number

The full series name and the number of the document should
come in parentheses after the imprint data (Fig. 7).

> U.S. Department of the Navy. Naval Historical Center.
> *On Course to Desert Storm: The United States Navy*
> *and the Persian Gulf* by Michael A. Palmer. Wash-
> ington: Government Printing Office, 1992. (Contri-
> butions to Naval History No. 5). (D207.10/4:5).

US 5.1a If a series number is given in the report number, you need not
repeat the report number in the series statement.

> U.S. Environmental Protection Agency. *Bioflocculation*
> *and the Accumulation of Chemicals by Floc-Forming*

> *Organisms* by Patrick R. Dugan (EPA-600/2-75-032). Washington: Government Printing Office, 1975. (Environmental Protection Technology Series). (EP1.23/2:600/2-75-032).

US 5.2   More Than One Series

When citing a series within a series, you must give both series' names.

> U.S. Bureau of the Census. *Voting and Registration in the Election of November 1982.* Washington: Government Printing Office, 1983. (Current Population Reports; P-20 Population Characteristics No. 383). (C3.186:P20/383).

US 6   NOTES

"Notes" is a catch-all category in which you can place significant information which does not fit in other segments of the citation. Anything included in notes should be in parentheses at the end of the citation. Depending upon the specific data, notes may or may not be required.

US 6.1   Required Notes

Required notes are those which would help your reader find *precisely* the same material you have in hand (e.g., a microform collection number; a *Serial Set* number; a Superintendent of Documents number, if available). Also required are indications about the publication which would affect the reader's ability to locate or use the information source (e.g., FOIA-obtained documents, unpublished papers, mimeographed items, distribution data, loose-leafs).

DISTRIBUTION DATA

> U.S. Air Force University. *Strategy for Defeat: The Luftwaffe 1933-1945* by Williamson Murray. Maxwell Air Force Base, Ala.: Air University Press, 1983. (Distributed by the Government Printing Office; D301.2:St7).

LOOSE-LEAF FORMAT

"Federal Employees Required To File Financial Disclosure Reports" (FPM Letter 734-1; 4 Nov. 1982). In U.S. Office of Personnel Management. *Federal Personnel Manual*. Washington: Government Printing Office. (Loose-leaf).

MICROFORM COLLECTION ENTRY NUMBERS

CIS Microfiche

U.S. Senate. *History of the Committee on Finance* (S.Doc.95-27). Washington: Government Printing Office, 1977. (1977 CIS microfiche S360-1).

Government Printing Office Microfiche

U.S. House. 97th Congress, 1st Session. *H.R. 3, A Bill To Amend the Internal Revenue Code of 1954. . . .* Washington: Government Printing Office, 1981. (GPO microfiche 10, coordinate D4).

Readex

U.S. Department of Health, Education and Welfare. *Management by Objectives: Planning Where To Go and How To Get There* by T.H. Bell. n.p., 1974. (1974 Readex non-dep. microcard 01191).

MIMEOGRAPHED DOCUMENTS (in-house documents)

U.S. Department of Education. *Investigation into Adolescent Promiscuity*. n.p., 1977. (Mimeo).

SERIAL SET VOLUME NUMBERS

U.S. House. Select Committee on Small Business. *Organization and Operation of the Small Business Administration: A Report . . . Pursuant to H.Res. 46 . . .* (H.Rpt.87-2564). Washington: Government Printing Office, 1963. (*Serial Set* 12440).

SUPERINTENDENT OF DOCUMENTS NUMBER (if known)

U.S. Smithsonian Institution. *Through Looking to Learning: The Museum Adventure* edited by Thomas E. Lowderbaugh. Washington: Smithsonian Institution Press, 1983. (SI.2:M97/6).

US 6.2   Optional Notes

Optional notes are those which would help your reader determine the quality of the document (e.g., poster, pamphlet, press release). Also optional is information about language or the size of non-print media (e.g., map scale or frame size).

LANGUAGE

> U.S. Department of Education. *MANA∂* by Elnora Mapatis. Washington: Government Printing Office, 1983. (Recounted in Hualapai).

MAP SCALE

> U.S. Geological Survey. *State College, Pa.* (map). Photorevised 1971. Washington: USGS, 1962. (1:2400).

PUBLICATION TYPE

> U.S. National Park Service. *Redwood.* Washington: Government Printing Office, 1990. (I29.2:R24/990; pamphlet and map).

US 7   CITING PARTS: ARTICLES, CHAPTERS, AND LOOSE-LEAFS

In citing a part of a publication (e.g., an article from a periodical, a chapter from a book, an insert from a hearing) you must use both the title of the part and the title of the whole. If you cite only the article, the reader will not be able to locate your source. If you cite only the source, the reader will not be able to locate the particular part that you considered relevant to your topic.

US 7.1   Periodicals

Periodicals (journals, magazines, newspapers, etc.) are publications issued with some frequency (more than once a year) whose titles do not change from issue to issue and whose contents include a variety of articles, stories, columns, editorials, notices, etc. Some examples are the *FBI Law Enforcement Bulletin*, *EPA Journal*, *Federal Register*, and *Congressional Record*.

A typical periodical citation includes the personal author of the article, the article's title, title of the periodical, volume and issue numbers, date, and pagination.

> Wallach, John M. "No More!" *All Hands* 905 (Aug. 1992) pp. 4-9. (D207.17:905).

US 7.1a Note that in some of the following periodical citations the issuing agency was included as a note. In most libraries and for most non-government periodicals you need to know only the name of the periodical to find it. This is not always true for government periodicals. Libraries which keep government documents separate from the rest of their collection may also keep government periodicals separate from other periodicals. Further, the standard catalogs of periodicals do not include all government periodicals. Including the name of the issuing agency in a note will help your reader locate an otherwise obscure title. This tells your readers to look in sources that list government periodicals.

> Cantor, Norman F. "Why Study the Middle Ages?" *Humanities* 3:3 (June 1982) pp. 21-30. (Issued by the U.S. National Endowment for the Humanities; NF3.11:3/3).

US 7.1b If the article has two authors, cite both; invert the name of the first author, so that the citation will file alphabetically in your bibliography. If there are more than three authors, cite the first one only and use "et al." or "and others" to cover the other authors (see US 2.6a).

> Greenburg, Martin A., and Ellen C. Wertleib. "The Police and the Elderly (Pt. II)," *FBI Law Enforcement Bulletin* 52:9 (Sept. 1983) pp. 1- 7. (J1.14/8:52/9).

US 7.1c If no author is listed for the article, start your citation with the article's title and omit the author segment of the citation.

> "Progress and Challenges: Looking at EPA Today," *EPA Journal* 16:5 (Sept/Oct. 1990) pp. 15-29. (EP1.67:16/5).

US 7.2 Non-periodicals

Usually when you cite a work, other than a periodical article, you cite the whole work. There are cases, however, where you might want to cite only a part of a work—a single paper in a collection of conference papers, a single article in an encyclopedic kind of source, or a piece of evidence inserted in a Congressional hearing. When to cite the whole work and when to cite only a part will depend on the purposes of your bibliography. How to cite a part will depend on the nature of the whole.

A citation to a part of any non-periodical publication is similar to a citation to the whole publication except that it is preceded by the part's author/title and by the range of pages, as appropriate.

CHAPTER IN A BOOK

Steiner, Richard. "Washington Present: Our Nation's Capitol Today," pp. 54-135. In U.S. Capitol Historical Society. *Washington Past and Present.* Washington: U.S. Capitol Historical Society, 1983.

CHAPTER IN AN ENCYCLOPEDIC SOURCE

"Engineers," pp. 64-72. In U.S. Bureau of Labor Statistics. *Occupational Outlook Handbook.* 1992-93 ed. Washington: Government Printing Office, 1992. (BLS Bulletin 2400).

MICROFICHE INSERTED IN PAPER TEXT

U.S. National Oceanic and Atmospheric Administration. "Determination of Petroleum Components in Samples from the Metula Oil Spill" by J. S. Warner (NOAA DR ERL MESA 4; microfiche). Boulder, Colo.: NOAA, 1976. In U.S. National Oceanic and Atmospheric Administration. *The Metula Oil Spill* by Charles G. Gunnerson and George Peter. Washington: Government Printing Office, 1976. (C55.602:M56).

PAPER IN CONFERENCE PROCEEDINGS

Park, Robert L. "The Muzzling of American Science," pp. 609-614. In U.S. House. Committee on Government Operations. *Computer Security Act of 1987* Hearing 25, 26 Feb. and 17 Mar. 1987. Washington: Government Printing Office, 1987. (Y4.G74/7:C43/29).

PAPER INSERTED IN A CONGRESSIONAL HEARING

Roberts, Steven V. "The Congress, the Press and the Public," pp. 183-198. In U.S. House. *Understanding Congress: Research Perspectives, The Papers and Commentary from "Understanding Congress: A Bicentennial Research Conference"* 9-10 Feb. 1989 (H.Doc.101-241). Washington: Government Printing Office, 1991. (Y1.1/7:101-241).

US 7.3 Loose-leafs

Some government publications come in loose-leaf format so that they can be easily updated. These are usually the procedural documents of the government bureaucracy—manuals, guidelines, regulations, standards, etc. They are often massive, and their internal organization may be complicated.

In citing these publications, you will usually be citing a specific part rather than the whole. The information to include will depend on the organization of the loose-leaf and will usually be the name of the part, the internal filing numbers, and a date. The date of the part to which you are referring is important, since it is entirely possible that the part you are citing will be superseded later by an amendment with the same number and name. The date will usually be printed at the top or bottom of each page.

Information about the volume or set should include: issuing agency, title, agency report number (if any), place, publisher, series number (if any), and "loose-leaf" in a note. You will note that the date of the main volume is omitted. If you can find an edition date for the whole publication, you may include it. However, it will be simply the date for the reprinted whole edition and will likely have later changes filed in.

Loose-leafs may be organized in many ways—by part number, by page number, or by some other system especially adapted to the contents of the loose-leaf. You must look at the publication and give the information that best locates the part you are citing.

LOOSE-LEAF ORGANIZED BY METHOD NUMBER

"Sampling for Inspection and Testing" (Method 1022; 1 Feb. 1980). In U.S. General Services Administration. *Paint, Varnish, Lacquer and Related Materials: Methods for Sampling and Testing.* Washington: Government Printing Office. (Federal Test Method Standard Number 141B). (Loose-leaf; GS2.8/7:141B).

LOOSE-LEAF ORGANIZED BY PAGE NUMBER

"Performance Funding System" (pp. 1-10; Feb. 1977). In U.S. Department of Housing and Urban Development. *Performance Funding System Handbook* (HUD Handbook 7475.13). Washington: HUD. (Loose-leaf; HH1.6/6:7475.13).

LOOSE-LEAF ORGANIZED BY SECTION NUMBER

"Telegraphic Bids" (Sect. 1-2.202-2 FPR Amendment 229; Mar. 1983). In U.S. General Services Administration. *Federal Procurement Regulations.* 2nd ed.; reprinted 1981. Washington: Government Printing Office. (Loose-leaf; GS1.6/5:964/rep.5).

US 8   SPECIAL CASES

Certain federal titles and some types of U.S. government documents are so frequently cited or present such unique problems that they require special rules. For your convenience they are discussed separately in this section. Many of these titles are so well known or appear in so many editions and formats that you can leave it to your reader to find a source. For this reason it is not necessary to include all citation elements.

Public Law
Number

Date of
Passage

Statute
Volume and
Page Number

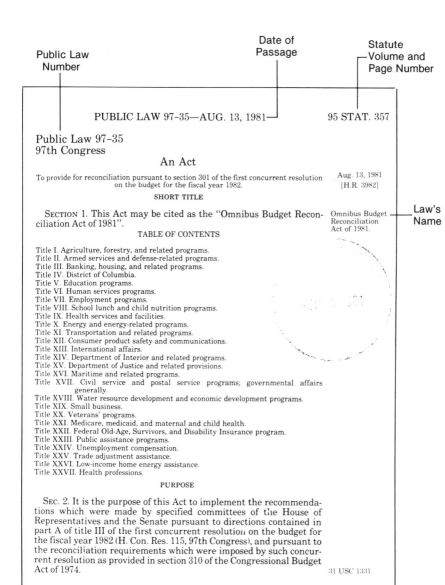

PUBLIC LAW 97–35—AUG. 13, 1981   95 STAT. 357

Public Law 97–35
97th Congress

An Act

To provide for reconciliation pursuant to section 301 of the first concurrent resolution on the budget for the fiscal year 1982.

Aug. 13, 1981
[H.R. 3982]

SHORT TITLE

SECTION 1. This Act may be cited as the "Omnibus Budget Reconciliation Act of 1981".

Omnibus Budget
Reconciliation
Act of 1981.

Law's
Name

TABLE OF CONTENTS

Title I. Agriculture, forestry, and related programs.
Title II. Armed services and defense-related programs.
Title III. Banking, housing, and related programs.
Title IV. District of Columbia.
Title V. Education programs.
Title VI. Human services programs.
Title VII. Employment programs.
Title VIII. School lunch and child nutrition programs.
Title IX. Health services and facilities.
Title X. Energy and energy-related programs.
Title XI. Transportation and related programs.
Title XII. Consumer product safety and communications.
Title XIII. International affairs.
Title XIV. Department of Interior and related programs.
Title XV. Department of Justice and related provisions.
Title XVI. Maritime and related programs.
Title XVII. Civil service and postal service programs; governmental affairs generally.
Title XVIII. Water resource development and economic development programs.
Title XIX. Small business.
Title XX. Veterans' programs.
Title XXI. Medicare, medicaid, and maternal and child health.
Title XXII. Federal Old-Age, Survivors, and Disability Insurance program.
Title XXIII. Public assistance programs.
Title XXIV. Unemployment compensation.
Title XXV. Trade adjustment assistance.
Title XXVI. Low-income home energy assistance.
Title XXVII. Health professions.

PURPOSE

SEC. 2. It is the purpose of this Act to implement the recommendations which were made by specified committees of the House of Representatives and the Senate pursuant to directions contained in part A of title III of the first concurrent resolution on the budget for the fiscal year 1982 (H. Con. Res. 115, 97th Congress), and pursuant to the reconciliation requirements which were imposed by such concurrent resolution as provided in section 310 of the Congressional Budget Act of 1974.

31 USC 1331.

Figure 8: First Page of a Law

US 8.1   **Constitution**

The U.S. Constitution can be found in many places. If citing the whole Constitution, give your source and its date. Since the Constitution has been amended over time, it may be important for the reader to know which version is being cited.

>   *The Constitution of the United States of America:
>   Analysis and Interpretation* (S.Doc.99-16). Washington: Government Printing Office, 1987. (*Serial Set* 13611).

US 8.1a   It is more likely that you will cite a part of the Constitution such as an article, a section, or an amendment. In this case, your source is not so important since numerous sources will contain precisely that part.

>   U.S. Constitution. Art. 1, Sect. 1.

US 8.2   **Government Manual**

The *U.S. Government Manual* is a product of the General Services Administration. However, since this title is a standard reference work, it is not necessary to include the name of the issuing agency. Simple citation to the item itself will suffice.

>   *United States Government Manual, 1991/92*. Washington: Government Printing Office, 1991.

US 8.3   **Statutes at Large**

To cite a public law found in the *Statutes at Large*, include the name of the law, its public law number (PL), date of passage, volume, and page numbers. The name of the law can usually be located in the first paragraph of the text or in the annotations on the side of the page (Fig. 8).

>   "Intermodel Surface Transportation Efficiency Act of
>   1991" (PL 102-240, 18 Dec. 1991), 105 *United
>   States Statutes at Large*, pp. 1914-2207.

US 8.3a   After passage, laws are first printed as pamphlets known as "slip laws." These can be cited by the name of the law, public law number, and date of passage.

"Higher Education Amendments of 1992" (PL 102-325, 23 July 1992).

US 8.4 U.S. Code (USC)

To cite a section of the *U.S. Code* give the name of the section, title number of the *U.S. Code*, the part number, and the year of the edition. Since the *U.S. Code* is constantly changing, the year of the edition is crucial.

"Community Mental Health Center," Title 42 *U.S. Code*, Pts. 2689 et seq. 1976 ed.

US 8.4a

The *U.S. Code* is updated annually by supplements for five years. The supplements are then incorporated into a new edition. When citing a section which appears in a supplement, give the original edition and the supplement number and its year.

"Vocational Rehabilitation Services," Title 29 *U.S. Code*, Pts. 720 et seq. 1976 ed. Supp. V, 1981.

US 8.5 Federal Register

To cite the *Federal Register* give the name of the section, any identifying agency report numbers, volume of the *Federal Register*, issue, date, and pagination. You should also include as part of the section name an indication of what action is represented (e.g., final rule, proposed rule to amend executive order, proclamation).

"Air Contaminants; Proposed Rule," 57 *Federal Register* 114 (12 June 1992), pp. 26002-26601.

US 8.6 Code of Federal Regulations (CFR)

To cite the *Code of Federal Regulations* give the name of the section, title number, *Code of Federal Regulations*, title and part numbers, and edition. Since the CFR is reissued annually and substantial regulatory changes may be enacted, inclusion of the edition statement is essential.

"Product Noise Labeling," Title 40 *Code of Federal Regulations*, Pt. 211. 1991 ed.

US 8.7   U.S. Reports

Give the full name of the case (plaintiff v. defendant), volume, *U.S. Reports*, date of the decision, and page numbers.

> Brown v. the Board of Education of Topeka, Shawnee County, Kansas, 347 *U.S. Reports* (17 May 1954) pp. 483-500.

US 8.8   Congressional Record

In citing the bound edition of the *Congressional Record* it is advisable to name the speaker, the title of the section, the volume number and part number of the *Record*, the date, and the pages cited. You need not include the Congress and session numbers since such information is superfluous. By giving the date of publication and volume/part number you have provided a check for your reader should a piece of data be inaccurately transposed. You should also identify the home state of the speaker. This may not seem important with unusual or famous names, but with common names such as Anderson or Smith, it can serve to distinguish two speakers for your reader.

> Rep. Anderson (Cal.). "Legislation for the Care of Vietnamese Refugees," *Congressional Record* 121, Pt. 10 (25 Apr. 1975) pp. 12-52.

Since the mid-1980s the bound *Congressional Record* has been distributed to most libraries as microfiche. To alert your readers to the fact that you used such a format, include a format note.

> Sen. Heinz (Pa.) "Protection of Victims and Witnesses of Crimes" *Congressional Record* (microfiche) 128, Pt. 9 (25 May 1982) p. 11621.

US 8.8a   For a general debate with several speakers, simply give the name of the section.

> "Religion and Schools," *Congressional Record* 20, Pt. 1 (21 Dec. 1888) pp. 433-434.

US 8.8b   In citing the daily edition of the *Congressional Record*, be sure to indicate that fact. The pagination in the daily edition changes once the item is included in a bound volume. Because of these changes, it is necessary to give sufficient information as to speaker, subject, date, etc. so that your reader can later locate the citation in the bound volumes.

> Sens. Hawkins (Fla.), Grassley (Ia.) and Packwood (Ore.). "Radio Marti," *Congressional Record* (12 Sept. 1983). Daily ed. S11970-11981.

US 8.9 **Congressional Globe, Register of Debates, and Annals of Congress**

The *Congressional Globe*, the *Register*, and the *Annals* are cited much like the *Congressional Record* (US 8.8), except that since there are no consistent volume numbers, the number of the Congress, the session number, and the part, if applicable, must be given. If there is no title, a descriptive statement can be used in its place.

ANNALS OF CONGRESS

> "Trial of Samuel Chase," *Annals of Congress* 8th Congress, 2nd Session (1804-1805) pp. 81-676.

CONGRESSIONAL GLOBE

> Sen. Polk (Mo.). Speech on the State of the Union, *Congressional Globe* 36th Congress, 2nd Session (14 Jan. 1861) Pt. 1, pp. 355-360.

CONGRESSIONAL GLOBE, APPENDIX

> Sen. Smith (Conn.). "Claims for French Spoliations," *Congressional Globe, Appendix* 31st Congress, 2nd Session (16 Jan. 1851) pp. 115-126.

REGISTER OF DEBATES

> "Gratitude to Lafayette," *Register of Debates* 18th Congress, 2nd Session (21 Dec. 1824) pp. 28-35.

US 8.10 **Journals of the Continental Congress**

There have been many editions of the *Journals*. How you cite them will depend upon the organization of the edition used. In every case the imprint (place, publisher, date) should be given. The Library of Congress edition is the most complete and most widely available. Its volumes are numbered consecutively; therefore, the volume number will locate an item precisely. However, it is a good idea to include the date of the Continental Congress in parentheses for your reader's convenience.

SINGLE ENTRY OR DOCUMENT WITHIN A VOLUME

"Address to the People of Great Britain," pp. 81-90. In U.S. Library of Congress. *Journals of the Continental Congress 1774-1789*, Vol. I (1774). Washington: Government Printing Office, 1904.

INDIVIDUAL VOLUME

U.S. Library of Congress. *Journals of the Continental Congress 1774-1789*, Vol. I (1774). Washington: Government Printing Office, 1904.

THE WHOLE SET

U.S. Library of Congress. *Journals of the Continental Congress 1774-1789*. Washington: Government Printing Office, 1904.

US 8.11 House (or Senate) Journal

Since titles are not usually given to sections of the *Journals*, just give the speaker, state, and subject. Then include Congress, session, date, and page numbers.

Albert, Carl (Okla.). Remarks, *Journal of the House of Representatives* 94th Congress, 1st Session (14 Jan. 1975) pp. 2-4.

US 8.12 Congressional Directory

The *Congressional Directory* is published once every Congress and is updated by a paper supplement. Since the title implies the issuing agency, it is not necessary to repeat the agency.

Congressional Directory, 1991-92. 102nd Congress. Washington: Government Printing Office, 1991.

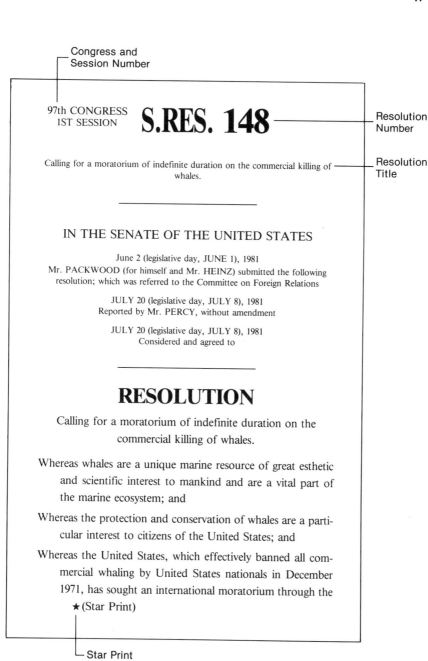

Congress and
Session Number

97th CONGRESS
1ST SESSION
S.RES. 148

Resolution
Number

Calling for a moratorium of indefinite duration on the commercial killing of whales.

Resolution
Title

IN THE SENATE OF THE UNITED STATES

June 2 (legislative day, JUNE 1), 1981
Mr. PACKWOOD (for himself and Mr. HEINZ) submitted the following resolution; which was referred to the Committee on Foreign Relations

JULY 20 (legislative day, JULY 8), 1981
Reported by Mr. PERCY, without amendment

JULY 20 (legislative day, JULY 8), 1981
Considered and agreed to

RESOLUTION

Calling for a moratorium of indefinite duration on the commercial killing of whales.

Whereas whales are a unique marine resource of great esthetic and scientific interest to mankind and are a vital part of the marine ecosystem; and

Whereas the protection and conservation of whales are a particular interest to citizens of the United States; and

Whereas the United States, which effectively banned all commercial whaling by United States nationals in December 1971, has sought an international moratorium through the

★(Star Print)

Star Print

Figure 9: U.S. Congressional Bill

US 8.13 Bills

For bills, resolutions, acts, and star prints, the issuing agency is either U.S. Senate or U.S. House, with no committee designation. These publications are issued by the entire Congressional chamber, not by a committee. You must also include the Congress and session number in the issuing agency statement (see US 1.3f).

US 8.13a The number of a bill or resolution is its most descriptive feature and should be used with the title. You may shorten the title from the text, if necessary (Fig. 9).

> U.S. House. 96th Congress, 1st Session. *H.R. 2, A Bill To Require Authorization for Budget Authority.* . . . Washington: Government Printing Office, 1979.

US 8.13b The legislative process may result in many amended versions of a bill or resolution, if a bill sees any action. Include either "Act" or "Star Print," as applicable, in the edition statement. An act is indicated in the bill's title. A star print is indicated by a small star on the lower left corner of the title page (Fig. 9).

> U.S. Senate. 97th Congress, 1st Session. *S.Res. 148, Resolution . . . for a Moratorium . . . on the Commercial Killing of Whales.* Star Print. Washington: Government Printing Office, 1982.

US 8.13c Since 1979 the GPO has been distributing bills and resolutions on microfiche; few institutions retain back files of these bills in paper form. Therefore, it is extremely likely that you will be citing, and your reader will be looking for, the microfiche edition. In order to facilitate location of the bill, you should include the fiche number and frame coordinates as a note.

> U.S. House. 102nd Congress, 1st Session. *H.R. 205, A Bill To Amend the Social Security Act* . . . Washington: Government Printing Office, 1991. (GPO microfiche 59, coordinate A3).

US 8.13d It is not unusual for a bill to be reprinted in its entirety in a hearing, report, or in the *Congressional Record*. If that is your text, cite it as part of the larger source.

> U.S. Senate. 94th Congress, 1st Session. "S.Res. 55, To Establish Legislative Review Subcommittees," *Congressional Record* 121, Pt. 2 (3 Feb. 1975) p. 2078.

US 8.14   Serial Set

The *U.S. Serial Set* is the official compilation of Congressional reports and documents. At one time nearly all government publications were issued as Congressional documents in the *Serial Set*. Thus, they all have a Congressional number (e.g., 42nd Congress, House Miscellaneous Doc. 242). The bound volumes have been numbered consecutively since 1817.

To cite material in the *Serial Set* you should give the Congress, session, title, and number (e.g., 58-2, House Report 21). If available also give imprint data. Inclusion of the *Serial Set* number is recommended and should be placed in a note.

> U.S. Senate. 50th Congress, 2nd Session. *Report on Indian Traderships* (S.Rpt.2707). Washington: Government Printing Office, 1899. (*Serial Set* 2623).

US 8.15   American State Papers

The *American State Papers (ASP)* is a compilation of the publications of the early Congresses, arranged in broad categories. With the *Serial Set* it forms the most complete collection available of Congressional reports and documents. Since the documents in *ASP* are not chronologically arranged, it is necessary to cite subject area, volume, report number, and page numbers.

> "Naval Register for 1832," *American State Papers: Naval Affairs*, Vol. IV (Doc. 461) pp. 48-63.

US 8.16   Foreign Relations of the United States

Foreign Relations of the United States, published since 1861, is a compilation of the diplomatic papers of the U.S. The set is arranged by year and within that year by volumes (and occasionally parts) which cover various geographic areas or policy issues. Due to classification and secrecy, these papers are not released for publication for many years; thus, the publication date will differ considerably from the year covered. Therefore, it is vital to your reader that you include both dates: one for locating and one for informational purposes.

> *Foreign Relations of the United States, 1949, Vol. VIII, Pt. 2: The Far East and Australia.* Washington: Government Printing Office, 1976.

US 8.16a To cite a single document within *Foreign Relations of the United States*:

> "The Secretary of State to the Embassy in Greece," pp. 533-534. In *Foreign Relations of the United States, 1951, Vol. V: The Near East and North Africa.* Washington: Government Printing Office, 1982.

US 8.16b Some volumes fall outside the annual series. These are compilations devoted to a single subject (Japan 1931-1941; Paris Peace Conference, 1919; etc.). In citations of these documents the name comes before the date of a volume number in the title to distinguish them from the annual compilations.

> *Foreign Relations of the United States: The Conferences at Washington, 1941-42, and Casablanca, 1943.* Washington: Government Printing Office, 1968.

US 8.17   Treaties

U.S. treaties are published in two forms: as individual documents in the *Treaties and Other International Acts (TIAS)* and in *United States Treaties (UST)*, the standard treaty compilation. In both they are arranged sequentially by TIAS number. You should cite the title, the parties, the date of signing, and the TIAS number. Other elements will depend on whether you are citing *TIAS* or *UST*.

Take the title from the first page of the treaty. Use the first form of agreement listed (e.g., treaty, convention, agreement), followed by a short title based on the subject matter. Since the U.S. is party to all treaties in these series, it is necessary to include only the other party in bilateral treaties and designate "multilateral" for multilateral treaties. Give the first and last dates of signing if there is more than one. Multilateral treaties may say "done at" rather than "signed." In any case use the date on the cover page of *TIAS*.

TIAS CITATION

> "Convention on Atomic Energy," Sweden, signed 27 Jan., 23 Feb. 1981, *Treaties and Other International Acts Series 10099.*

UST CITATION

> "General Agreement on Tariffs and Trade," done 10 Mar. 1955, multilateral (TIAS 3437), *United States Treaties* 6, Pt. 5 (1955) p. 5815.

US 8.18 Weekly Compilation of Presidential Documents

The *Weekly Compilation* can be cited like a typical periodical. The title should include the title of the article, nature of the document (e.g., speech, executive order, proclamation), and the date of the document.

> "Introduction of Illegal Aliens" (Executive Order 12807, 29 May 1992), *Weekly Compilation of Presidential Documents* 28:22 (1 June 1992) pp. 923-924.

US 8.18a If the nature of the document and its date are given in the title, they do not need to be repeated.

> "The President's News Conference of October 19, 1983," *Weekly Compilation of Presidential Documents* 19:42 (24 Oct. 1983) pp. 1465-1472.

US 8.19 Public Papers of the Presidents

The bound compilations of Presidential documents are arranged by President, year, and volume number (if there is more than one volume in the year). As in standard sources, the title should be first and then the President's name. Since there are other non-governmental editions available, it is necessary to include imprint data.

A SINGLE DOCUMENT

"Inaugural Address" (20 Jan. 1961), pp. 1-3. In *Public Papers of the Presidents of the United States: John F. Kennedy, 1961.* Washington: Government Printing Office, 1962.

ALL THE VOLUMES OF A PRESIDENT

Public Papers of the Presidents of the United States: John F. Kennedy. Washington: Government Printing Office, 1962-1964.

A SINGLE VOLUME OF A PRESIDENT

Public Papers of the Presidents of the United States: John F. Kennedy, 1961. Washington: Government Printing Office, 1962.

A NON-GOVERNMENT EDITION

The Public Papers and Addresses of Franklin D. Roosevelt. New York: Random House, 1938-1950.

US 8.20 Economic Report of the President

The *Economic Report of the President* appears in two editions each year: the Congressional and the executive branch version. The Congressional version will have a House document number.

CONGRESSIONAL VERSION

Economic Report of the President February 1992 (H.Doc.102-177). Washington: Government Printing Office, 1992.

EXECUTIVE BRANCH VERSION

Economic Report of the President February 1992. Washington: Government Printing Office, 1992.

US 8.21 Budget of the United States

The *Budget of the United States* appears in two editions: Congressional and executive branch. To differentiate between the two, look for the Congressional numbering scheme on the document.

CONGRESSIONAL VERSION

> *Budget of the United States Fiscal Year 1993* (H.Doc. 102-178). Washington: Government Printing Office, 1992.

EXECUTIVE BRANCH VERSION

> *Budget of the United States Fiscal Year 1993.* Washington: Government Printing Office, 1992.

US 8.22 Census

The U.S. Census is extremely complex and may require varying pieces of information for any citation. The key is to include enough information so that your reader can locate a volume or part of the census.

You should always include the complete title and census year of the report being cited; any edition and volume statements; and the place, publisher, and date of publication. The inclusion of these data will help differentiate the volumes of the census published both by the government and by the private sector.

> *U.S. Census, 1790: Heads of Families.* Washington: Government Printing Office, 1908.

US 8.22a Include a personal author if one is named.

> *U.S. Census, 1850: Statistical View of the United States . . . Compendium of the Seventh Census* by J. D. B. DeBow. Washington: A.O.P. Nicholson, Public Printer, 1854.

US 8.22b In the early censuses statistics on manufacturers, agriculture, housing, population, etc. were taken as part of the decennial census. Gradually various economic questions came to be covered in separate censuses. The first element in a citation to a modern census should be the type and year of the census. The name of the census should be taken directly from the publication. Include any volume numbers given before the title of the specific document.

> *U.S. Census of Manufacturers, 1967: Vol. II, Industry Statistics: Pt. I Major Groups 20-24. Final Report.* Washington: Government Printing Office, 1971.

US 8.22c   If a census report number is given (usually on the upper left or right corner of the title/cover page), use it in the title statement.

> *U S. Census of Population, 1970: Subject Reports: American Indians* (PC(2)-IF). Final Report. Washington: Government Printing Office, 1973.

US 8.22d   The GPO has issued parts of the census on microfiche. When you cite the census in a format other than paper, you should include the medium as a part of the title statement (see US 2.9).

> *U.S. Census of Population and Housing, 1980: Block Statistics: Minnesota, Selected Areas* (PHC 80-1-25; microfiche). Washington: Government Printing Office, 1982. (C3.229/5:PHC80-1-25).

US 8.22e   Today electronic resources are being used extensively by the U.S. Bureau of the Census to disseminate information. See Chapter 6 for further discussion.

US 8.22f   If applicable, you should specify when you are citing a preliminary, advance, or final report. This is basically an edition statement and should be placed appropriately.

> *U.S. Census of Population and Housing, 1980: Final Population and Housing Unit Counts Pennsylvania* (PHC 80-V-40). Advance Report. Washington: Government Printing Office, 1982.

> *U.S. Census of Population and Housing, 1990: Summary Social Economic, and Housing Characteristics Virginia 1990* (CPH-5-48). Final Report. Washington: Government Printing Office, 1992.

US 8.22g   Much of the data of the census has been reproduced and sold by groups other than the federal government. If you use such a source, be sure to inform your reader in the imprint data that you did not use the government version of a census or census data. This is very important since frequently in these publications the data has been manipulated or sorted to appear in certain groupings which are not in the official census.

COMMERCIAL PUBLISHER

1980 U.S. Census Population and Housing Characteristics: Place Data and Indexes. San Diego: National Decision Systems, 1982.

STATE DATA CENTER PUBLICATION

Pennsylvania Municipalities: 1980 General Population and Housing Characteristics (PSDE 80-1-82). Middletown, Pa.: Pennsylvania State Data Center, 1982.

US 8.23 Statistical Abstract of the United States

One of the most enduring government documents and one of the most frequently used reference sources, the *Statistical Abstract* can be cited by giving title, edition, and imprint.

Statistical Abstract of the United States, 1991. 111th ed. Washington: Government Printing Office, 1991.

US 8.23a If citing a specific table or data set from the book, give the name and number of the table followed by the pagination.

"Boy Scouts and Girl Scouts—Membership and Units: 1970 to 1989," No. 410, p. 241. In *Statistical Abstract of the United States, 1991.* 111th ed. Washington: Government Printing Office, 1991.

US 8.24 Patents

To cite a patent granted by the U.S. government, you will probably have in hand either the patent itself or its abstract in the *Official Gazette*. In either case it is recommended that you give your reader the name of the invention, the inventor, the patent number, and the date granted. A citation to the abstract will also include a citation into the correct volume of the *Official Gazette*.

PATENT

"Implement Wheel" by William Schumacher. U.S. Patent 4,376,554 (15 Mar. 1983).

OFFICIAL GAZETTE
> "Implement Wheel" by William Schumacher. U.S. Patent 4,376,554 (15 Mar. 1983), *Official Gazette of the United States Patent and Trademark Office* 1028:3 (15 Mar. 1983) p. 517.

US 8.25   Joint Publications Research Service (JPRS) Reports

JPRS reports are primarily translations of print media. Usually several articles are grouped in each report, and the reports are grouped by geographic area. Information on the original source is found in the paragraph heading for each translation. For the microfiche edition you will have to look at the first frame of the translation to find this information. You should include personal author (if any), the title (shortened if necessary), the city and source of the original document, volume, date, and page numbers. When an entire book is translated, you should include all of the following (if given): author, translated title, original title, place, publisher, and date.

The second part of the citation describes the JPRS series. You should include the area name and report number (if they are given), the JPRS report number, and the date of the translation. This information can be found on the title page, the bibliographic data sheet, or on the microfiche header. In citing a GPO microfiche edition (the most widely used), give the microfiche number if there is more than one microfiche per report, and the page numbers on the microfiche. Finally, your citation should include a note containing either the SuDoc number or the Readex entry number.

PERIODICAL CITATION IN THE GPO EDITION
> Konstandinou, T.S. "PASOK Positions on EEC Membership Analyzed," Athens *Oikonomikos Takhydromas* 46 (12 Nov. 1981) pp. 23-26. Translation by the Joint Publications Research Service. *West Europe Report No. 1885*, JPRS No. 79843; 12 Jan. 1982. (GPO microfiche; PrEx7.18:1885; pp. 25-35).

Page Number

Title of Original

Paragraph Headings

Text of Translation

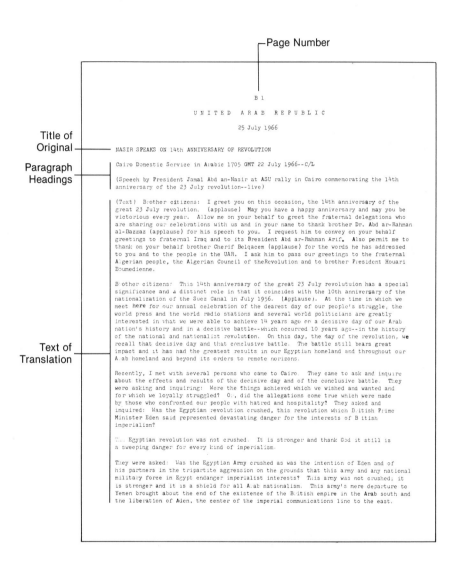

B 1

UNITED ARAB REPUBLIC

25 July 1966

NASIR SPEAKS ON 14th ANNIVERSARY OF REVOLUTION

Cairo Domestic Service in Arabic 1705 GMT 22 July 1966--C/L

(Speech by President Jamal Abd an-Nasir at ASU rally in Cairo commemorating the 14th anniversary of the 23 July revolution--live)

(Text) Brother citizens: I greet you on this occasion, the 14th anniversary of the great 23 July revolution. (applause) May you have a happy anniversary and may you be victorious every year. Allow me on your behalf to greet the fraternal delegations who are sharing our celebrations with us and in your name to thank brother Dr. Abd ar-Rahman al-Bazzaz (applause) for his speech to you. I request him to convey on your behalf greetings to fraternal Iraq and to its President Abd ar-Rahman Arif. Also permit me to thank on your behalf brother Cherif Belqacem (applause) for the words he has addressed to you and to the people in the UAR. I ask him to pass our greetings to the fraternal Algerian people, the Algerian Council of theRevolution and to brother President Houari Boumedienne.

Brother citizens: This 14th anniversary of the great 23 July revolutuion has a special significance and a distinct role in that it coincides with the 10th anniversary of the nationalization of the Suez Canal in July 1956. (Applause). At the time in which we meet here for our annual celebration of the dearest day of our people's struggle, the world press and the world radio stations and several world politicians are greatly interested in what we were able to achieve 14 years ago on a decisive day of our Arab nation's history and in a decisive battle--which occurred 10 years ago--in the history of the national and nationalist revolution. On this day, the day of the revolution, we recall that decisive day and that conclusive battle. The battle still bears great impact and it has had the greatest results in our Egyptian homeland and throughout our Arab homeland and beyond its orders to remote norizons.

Recently, I met with several persons who came to Cairo. They came to ask and inquire about the effects and results of the decisive day and of the conclusive battle. They were asking and inquiring: Were the things achieved which we wished and wanted and for which we loyally struggled? Or, did the allegations come true which were made by those who confronted our people with hatred and hospitality? They asked and inquired: Was the Egyptian revolution crushed, this revolution which British Prime Minister Eden said represented devastating danger for the interests of B itish imperialism?

The Egyptian revolution was not crushed. It is stronger and thank God it still is a sweeping danger for every kind of imperialism.

They were asked: Was the Egyptian Army crushed as was the intention of Eden and of his partners in the tripartite aggression on the grounds that this army and any national military force in Egypt endanger imperialist interests? This army was not crushed; it is stronger and it is a shield for all Arab nationalism. This army's mere departure to Yemen brought about the end of the existence of the British empire in the Arab south and the liberation of Aden, the center of the imperial communications line to the east.

Figure 10: FBIS Report Page

BOOK CITATION IN READEX EDITION

> *Subversion: Uruguayan Armed Forces Summary of
> Subversive Movements in Latin America* (trans. of *La
> Subversion*). Montevideo: Joint Chiefs of Staff,
> Uruguayan Armed Forces, 1977. Translation by the
> Joint Publications Research Service. JPRS No.
> 69596-1; 12 Aug. 1977. (1978 Readex microprint
> 12212).

US 8.26   Foreign Broadcast Information Service (FBIS) Reports

The FBIS reports are translations of written and spoken
media messages picked up by FBIS bureaus located throughout the world. These messages are usually translated from a
foreign language into English, although occasionally the
television/radio transmissions are made initially in English.
The reports themselves group these translations by geopoliti-
cal source and subject area. In citing an FBIS document take
the information about the original document from the paragraph heading (Fig. 10).

US 8.26a   For newspaper accounts the citation will be the same as JPRS
citations: personal author, if any; title; an edition statement as
to whether the translation is complete text or only excerpts;
city and source; volume; date; and page number. This is then
followed by a citation to the FBIS report which includes
name, volume, issue, date, any locational notes, and pagination in the report.

> Simurov, A. and V. Yanovskiy. "We Have Come To
> Know Each Other Better; the Peace March-82 Has
> Ended" (text). Moscow *Pravda* (30 July 1982) p. 4.
> Translation by the Foreign Broadcast Information
> Service. *FBIS Daily Report—Soviet Union* Vol. III:
> 150; 4 Aug. 1982 (GPO microfiche;
> PrEx7.10:FBIS-SOV-82-150; pp. AA7-11).

US 8.26b   For television/radio broadcasts include personal author, title,
edition statement (as above), the source and language in
which the message was broadcast, and the date of broadcast
in Greenwich Mean Time (GMT). All of this information is
given in a line (or more) which precedes the translation. This

is followed by a citation covering the FBIS report in which the translation can be found, including the SuDoc number if available.

MICROFICHE COPY

> Mnatsakonov, Edward. "The World Today" (text). Moscow Domestic Television Service in Russian, 1445 GMT 3 Aug. 1982. Translation by the Foreign Broadcast Information Service. *FBIS Daily Report— Soviet Union* Vol. III:150; 4 Aug. 1982. (GPO microfiche; PrEx7.10:FBIS-SOV-82-150; p. H14).

PAPER COPY

> "Destroyer Sent to Beirut" (excerpts). Rome Domestic Service in Italian, 2200 GMT 9 May 1983. Translation by the Foreign Broadcast Information Service. *FBIS Daily Report—Western Europe* Vol. VII:91; 10 May 1983; p. A7.

US 8.27   Securities and Exchange Commission Reports

The Securities and Exchange Commission requires various financial reports from companies selling stock on national exchanges. These reports vary in periodicity and content. The best known is the annual 10-K report, but there are, among others, 10-Q's, 8-K's, and 10-C's. These reports are all filed with the SEC, and some are official company reports sent to stockholders. All of them are filmed by private micro-publishers. In citing one of these reports authorship should be given to the company producing the report. The title, short-ened if possible, should then follow. If you are citing the paper version of the report, imprint data should include the year of filing and the location of corporate headquarters.

> Ford Corporation. *Form 10-K Annual Report . . . FY Ended Dec. 31, 1991.* Detroit, Mich., 1992.

US 8.27a In citing a micropublisher's version of the report, include the micropublisher's filming date and name in a note following the main part of the citation.

> Ford Corporation. *Form 10-K Annual Report . . . FY Ended Dec. 31, 1991.* Detroit, Mich., 1992. (1992 Disclosure microfiche).

US 8.28   Clearinghouse Documents

The U.S. government has established more than 300 clearing-houses that gather and distribute information on various topics. Clearinghouse documents may be unpublished reports, contract reports, or reports previously published by non-governmental and governmental organizations at all levels. These documents are generally known as technical reports, although their subject matter is frequently neither scientific nor technical.

US 8.28a   A citation to a contract report should include, as applicable: sponsoring agency, title, personal author, institutional affiliation and location, report number, date, and a note including the abbreviated clearinghouse name and the report identification number (Fig. 5). If the medium is other than paper, it should be noted (see also US 8.28e).

> U.S. Environmental Protection Agency. Office of Research and Development. *Evaluation of Solid Sorbents for Water Sampling* by J. C. Harris et al. of Arthur D. Little, Inc., Cambridge, Mass. (EPA-600/2-80-193). 1980. (NTIS PB 81-106585).

US 8.28b   A citation to a government report should include, as applicable: issuing agency, title, personal authors (if any), imprint, series, and a note including the abbreviated clearinghouse name and the report identification number. If the medium is other than paper, it should be noted.

> U.S. Department of Health, Education and Welfare. Bureau of Occupational and Adult Education. *Counseling Implications of Re-Entry Women's Life Experiences* by Ruth Ekstrom et al. Washington: DHEW, 1980. (ERIC microfiche ED 209 600).

US 8.28c   A citation to a non-governmental report should include, as applicable: personal author, title, imprint, series, and a note including the abbreviated clearinghouse name and the report identification number. If the medium is other than paper, it should be noted.

> Greeley, Andrew M. *The Rediscovery of Diversity.*
> Chicago: National Opinion Research Center, 1971.
> (ERIC microfiche ED 068 602).

US 8.28d A citation to an unpublished report should include, as applicable: personal author, title, date, and a note including the abbreviated clearinghouse name and report identification number. If the medium is other than paper, it should be noted.

> Basefsky, Stuart. *Bibliographic Citations and U.S.*
> *Government Publications.* 1979. (ERIC microfiche
> ED 223 251).

US 8.28e Some contract reports are distributed both by the GPO and by clearinghouses. If you have a document distributed by GPO (see US 4.2) which also has a clearinghouse availability statement, you should alert your reader in a note to this dual distribution (Fig. 5).

> U.S. National Aeronautics and Space Administration.
> *Environmental Exposure Effects on Composite*
> *Materials for Commercial Aircraft* by Martin N.
> Gibbons and Daniel J. Hoffman of Advanced Structures, Boeing Commercial Airplane Co., Seattle,
> Wash. (NASACR-3502; microfiche). Washington:
> Government Printing Office, 1982. (NAS1.26:3502;
> also available NTIS NASA-CR-3502).

US 8.29 **Commercial Publication Reprints as Federal Documents**

The federal government infrequently distributes documents which have not been issued or written by an agency. In these cases an agency has partially sponsored the writing or development of the document, and the government reprints and distributes the commercial publication.

For such documents a citation to the item should include the personal author, title, edition, imprint, and series data, as applicable. Since there may be no straightforward indication that the government had any connection with the production of the document, a distribution and Superintendent of Documents classification note should be added alerting your reader that the item is also a government document.

UNIVERSITY PRESS BOOK

> Shigo, Alex and Karl Roy. *Violin Woods*: *A New Look*.
> Durham, N.H.: University of New Hampshire, 1983.
> (Distributed by GPO; A13.2:V81).

PRIVATE PUBLISHER REPRINT

> Quirk, James, Katsuaki Terasawa, and David Whipple.
> *Coal Models and Their Use in Government Planning*.
> New York: Praeger, 1982. (Distributed by GPO;
> NAS1.2:C63).

US 8.30   Microform Collections

Several commercial publishers distribute federal documents republished in microform and organized into collections. If you are using a document from such a collection, you must cite both the original document and the microform collection. The first part of the citation should contain a complete reference to the original paper document, taken from the title page frame of the microform. The information about the collection should be given in a note at the end. What information is given will depend on the organization of the collection. Use whatever information you used to locate the document in the microform collection.

US 8.30a   Some collections are organized by year and by a filing control number assigned by the publisher.

> U.S. Department of Health, Education and Welfare. *The Measure of Poverty*. Washington: DHEW, 1976. (1976 ASI microfiche 4006-3).

US 8.30b   Some collections follow the organization of the source from which they were filmed. The Greenwood Press microfiche collection was filmed from the Senate Library and uses the Senate volume number as an accession number. Since several documents may be found in one volume, you should also include the "tab" number for location on the microfiche. The tab is the numbered frame preceding the document on the microfiche.

> U.S. Senate. Committee on Labor and Public Welfare. *Mine Safety Hearings* 18-19, 24-27, 31 May 1949. Washington: Government Printing Office, 1949. (81st Congress Greenwood Press microfiche S. Vol. 908-1).

US 8.31   Archives and Documents

Some government documents are not published in the traditional sense and are available only in archives. To cite such documents, follow the general rules outlined in US1-US7 and include a note informing your reader about the collection, box number and the location of the document.

> Garfield, James A. Correspondence to Lucretia Garfield. September 14, 1868. (James A. Garfield Papers; Box 3; Library of Congress Manuscript Division, Washington, DC).

US 8.31a   Frequently archival material is microfilmed as part of a subject-based collection. In citing such a document you must cite the microform collection as well as the document, since it is unlikely that your reader would ever find it except in that specific microform collection. This is in contrast to a republication of a popular or current title on microform by a private publisher, such as CIS (see US 8.30). Give the issuing agency, title (shortened if necessary), place, and date of issuance for the original document. Then give the title and imprint of the collection and whatever number (e.g., reel number, microfiche number) is used to locate the document.

MICROFICHE COLLECTION OF A COMMERCIAL PUBLISHER

> U.S. Joint Chiefs of Staff. *Memorandum for the Deputy Director for Intelligence . . . [on] Development of U.S. Position on Zones of Occupation for Germany, 1943-44.* Washington: 1952. In *Declassified Documents Reference System, 1980.* Washington: Carrolton Press, 1980. (Microfiche 42A).

MICROFILM COLLECTION OF A COMMERCIAL PUBLISHER

> U.S. Library of Congress. Congressional Research Service. *Do We Really Need All Those Electric Plants?* by Alvin Kaufman and Karen K. Nelson. 1982. In *Major Studies and Issue Briefs of the Congressional Research Service, 1982-83 Supp.* Frederick, Md: University Publications of America, 1983. (Reel IV, frame 278).

MICROFILM COLLECTION BY A GOVERNMENT AGENCY

> U.S. Census of Population, 1900. Schedule No. 1: Allen Township, Northhampton County, Pennsylvania. In U.S. National Archives and Records Service. *Twelfth Census of the United States, 1900.* Washington: NARS, 1973. (Reel 1446).

MICROFICHE COLLECTION BY A GOVERNMENT AGENCY (see also US 8.28)

> U.S. National Bureau of Standards. Center for Fire Research. *Effect of Ventilation on the Rates of Heat, Smoke and Carbon Monoxide Production in a Typical Jail Cell Fire* by B.T. Lee. Washington, 1982. In U.S. National Criminal Justice Reference Service. *Microfiche Collection* (NCJ-84592).

US 8.32   Freedom of Information Act (FOIA)

For documents obtained under the Freedom of Information Act (FOIA), you should try to identify the documents as precisely as possible. The element used will depend on the nature of the document and the amount of information given. Some elements which should be included are: personal author and agency affiliation; title or subject; type of document, including identifying numbers or other information; date; and number of pages.

You should also name the agency from which you obtained the document, the nature of your request, the date of your request, and the date of receipt. With this information your reader could (theoretically) get the same documents.

LETTER

> Hamilton, Donald R. U.S. Embassy, El Salvador.
> [Subject: Roatan Island]. Letter to Stephen Dachi,
> U.S. Information Agency; 2 Mar. 1983. 2 pp. Ob-
> tained under the Freedom of Information Act from
> U.S. Information Agency; requested as "Materials on
> Radio Marti" May 1983; received June 1983.

FORM (contract, requisition, etc.)

> 50 KW Antenna Design and Proposed Site Evaluation,
> Antigua, W.I. Request for Supplies/Service; Order
> No. A226842; 24 May 1982. 7 pp. Obtained under
> the Freedom of Information Act from U.S. Informa-
> tion Agency; requested as "Materials on Radio
> Marti," May 1983; received June 1983.

MEMORANDUM

> Fernandez, John. Conference by High-Ranking State
> Department Officials on Radio Marti and the
> Hawkins Bill (S. 602). Memorandum to Shay,
> Rodriguez and Briss; 4 Mar. 1983. 3 pp. Obtained
> under the Freedom of Information Act from U.S.
> Information Agency; requested as "Materials on
> Radio Marti" May 1983; received June 1983.

PAPER (no author given, no date)

> Assessment of the Effect of Radio Free Cuba (RFC) on
> the Second Session, Region 11 Medium Frequency
> Broadcasting Conference, Rio de Janeiro, Nov. 1981.
> Working paper. n.d. 2 pp. Obtained under the Free-
> dom of Information Act from U.S. Information
> Agency; requested as "Materials on Radio Marti,"
> May 1983; received June 1983.

PAPER (no author, omissions noted; date implied by text)

> VOA Requirements in the Caribbean. Position Paper No.
> 5C [missing pages]. [1981?]. 6 pp. Obtained under
> the Freedom of Information Act from U.S. Informa-
> tion Agency; requested as "Materials on Radio
> Marti," May 1983; received June 1983.

TELEGRAM (include, if given, reference numbers, time, sender, and receiver)

> International Telecommunications Union. Plenipotentiary Conference Nairobi . . . 952Z 5 Nov. 1982, 10322 (incoming telegram NAIROB28119). 3 pp. Obtained under the Freedom of Information Act from U.S. Department of State; requested as "Materials on Radio Marti," May 1983; received June 1983.

REPORT (include identifying number)

> Castro on Radio Marti. 19 Aug. 1982 (Correspondent Rpt. #2-8806). 1 p. Obtained under the Freedom of Information Act from U.S. Information Agency; requested as "Materials on Radio Marti," May 1983; received June 1983.

3

State, Local, and Regional Government Information Resources

State, local, and regional (SLR) documents are publications either written or funded by a governmental entity. State/territorial documents tend to be produced by all branches of the fifty state governments and U.S. territories. Local and regional documents generally are products of city councils, county governments, and economic or planning commissions. Usually SLR documents are not produced in great quantity and are not uniformly distributed; thus, locating them can be a major problem to the researcher. Consequently, any citation elements which facilitate location should be included.

SLR 1   ISSUING AGENCY

Just as for U.S. documents, use the issuing agency as the first element for an SLR document citation. The rationale for citing the agency is:

1) indexing in the major reference sources lists documents by issuing agencies (see Appendix B);
2) indicating that you are dealing with an SLR document may facilitate its location in a library, since these documents frequently are housed in separate library collections;
3) since many state and local agencies have no formal distribution program, crediting the agency may help your reader acquire the document from the appropriate agency.

SLR 1.1   Geographic/Political Designation

For any local, state, or territorial document the issuing agency statement should begin with the complete name of the geographic/political entity issuing the report. This can be abbreviated. Care should be taken that sufficient information is given so that geographic/political entities with similar names (e.g., Beaufort, N.C. and Beaufort, S.C.) are distinguishable.

LOCAL

> Allentown, Pa. Urban Observatory. *An Analysis of Tire Service Delivery for Master Planning in Allentown, Pa. 1977.*

STATE

> Idaho. Transportation Department. *A Guide to Abandoned Vehicles.* Boise, n.d.

TERRITORY

> Northern Mariana Islands. Coastal Resources Managment Office. *Suspended Sediment Load Study at Saipan Lagoon.* Saipan, 1989.

SLR 1.1a For regional documents the citation should begin with the name of the issuing agency. If the region is within one state, end this statement with a standard state abbreviation in parentheses.

> Centre Regional Planning Commission (Pa.). *Prospects for Industrial Zoning.* State College, 1969. (Land Use Study 1).

SLR 1.1b If the state's name appears as part of the agency's name, omit the state abbreviation at the end.

> Southwestern Pennsylvania Planning Commission. *The Plan for the 80s.* Pittsburgh, 1979.

SLR 1.1c For regional organizations which cross state boundaries, the inclusion of a single geographic designation in this statement is impossible. Location of these organizations is found in the imprint (see SLR 4.1c).

> Colorado River Basin Salinity Control Forum. *Report on the 1990 Review: Water Quality Standards for Salinity, Colorado River System.* Bountiful, Utah, 1990.

SLR 1.2   Single Issuing Agency

> Since local and state governments are constantly altering bureaucratic form and changing names, it is best to include in your citation all the hierarchical levels listed on the document, going from the largest to the smallest. This will help your reader to find an agency in the standard reference sources (Appendix B) and may locate a document if a name change has occurred.

> LOCAL

>> New York, N.Y. Department of Transportation. Bureau of Highway Operations. *1982 Annual Condition Report on Bridges and Tunnels.* 1983.

> STATE

>> Minnesota. Pollution Control Agency. *MEPA Hazardous Waste Compliance Guide.* St. Paul, 1991.

SLR 1.2a For regional documents give the complete name of the agency, ending with an abbreviated state designation, as appropriate (see SLR 1.1a and b).

> Joint Planning Commission of Lehigh-Northampton Counties (Pa.). *Population Growth Trends, 1980.* Lehigh Valley, 1981.

SLR 1.2b Some SLR documents do not list an issuing agency on the cover or the title page. This frequently occurs on mimeographed documents or computerized printouts. If you are using such a document, it is best to give your reader an idea of the agency issuing the report, assuming you know it or can at least give an educated guess. In such a case, bracket the issuing agency's name. If you do not know the source, omit the agency statement and simply begin your citation with the title (see SLR 2.1).

> [Idaho. Department of Education.] *Fall Enrollment Report, 1982/83.* Boise, 1982.

SLR 1.3   Multiple Issuing Agencies

> Sometimes more than one political body may be instrumental in the production of a document, as in a cooperative effort

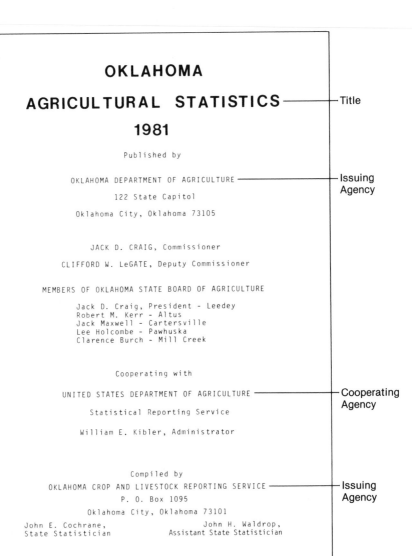

Figure 11: State Document Title Page

between a federal and a state/local agency (Fig. 11). Use the first agency listed as the issuing agency. If you feel acknowledgment of the cooperative effort is a significant fact, this can be included in a note (see SLR 6.2).

> Oklahoma. Department of Agriculture. Crop and Livestock Reporting Service. *Oklahoma Agricultural Statistics 1981*. Oklahoma City, 1982. (Produced as a cooperative effort with the U.S. Dept. of Agriculture).

SLR 1.4   Legislature as an Issuing Agency

All states have a legislative body in their governmental structure. The names of these entities differ (e.g., General Assembly, Legislature, Legislative Assembly), but the work done is the same (see SLR 8.5). Citing such documents first requires identification of the geographic area and the name of the entity.

> South Carolina. General Assembly. House of Representatives. *Annual Report, 1989/90*. Columbia, 1990.

SLR 1.4a If the document is a product of a legislative chamber, committee, or group, this should be noted in the agency statement.

> California. Legislature. Assembly. Committee on Revenue and Taxation. *Alcohol Beverage Taxation: A Briefing Book* by David Doerr (874). Sacramento, 1981.

SLR 1.4b If the document is a piece of legislation, the session, assembly, or meeting number should be included as part of the agency statement. Use this information as it appears on the document.

> Pennsylvania. General Assembly. Session of 1992. *Senate Bill No. 1639, An Act . . . Welfare Laws of the Commonwealth* (Printer's No. 2025). Harrisburg, 1992.

SLR 2   **TITLE**

The problems in locating titles for SLR documents are similar to those outlined for U.S. documents (see US 2). An additional problem can be the complete absence of any title. Such documents are often mimeographed documents copied in a very limited number for in-house purposes and not published for general distribution.

SLR 2.1   **Location of Title**

The procedure for locating an SLR title is similar to that for U.S. documents (see US 2.1). Look at the title page, the cover, and/or the spine of the document, as appropriate. Choose the boldest statement of title. If the title and cover page differ, use the title page information since this is the page used by indexers. If there is a bibliographic data sheet (Fig.12), use the information listed there.

> Minnesota. Department of Economic Development. Research Division. *Minnesota Statistical Profile 1992*. St. Paul, 1992.

SLR 2.1a If there is no obvious title, devise a descriptive title and put it in brackets.

> Montana. Department of Community Affairs. Division of Research and Information Systems. [Profiles: Pondera County] (computer printout). 3rd ed. Helena, 1978.

SLR 2.1b If you are using a document on microfiche, be sure to use the title as it appears on the document; do not rely on the fiche header.

> Minnesota. Division of Fish and Wildlife. *1981 Big Game Hunting Regulations* (microfiche). St. Paul, 1981.

SLR 2.2   **Subtitles**

Include a subtitle if it further defines or differentiates the subject of the document:

Title ————

Issuing
Agency

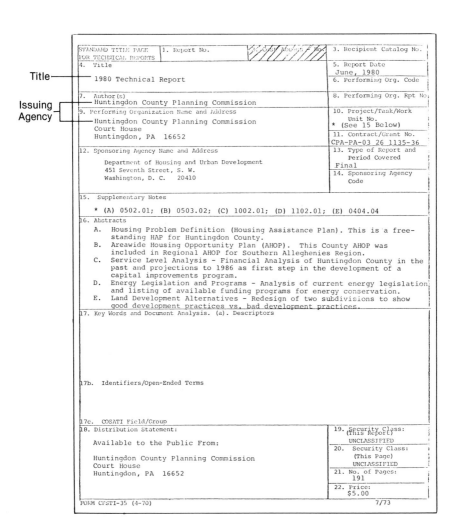

STANDARD TITLE PAGE FOR TECHNICAL REPORTS	1. Report No.		3. Recipient Catalog No.
4. Title 1980 Technical Report			5. Report Date June, 1980
			6. Performing Org. Code
7. Author(s) Huntingdon County Planning Commission			8. Performing Org. Rpt No.
9. Performing Organization Name and Address Huntingdon County Planning Commission Court House Huntingdon, PA 16652			10. Project/Task/Work Unit No. * (See 15 Below)
			11. Contract/Grant No. CPA-PA-03 26 1135-36
12. Sponsoring Agency Name and Address Department of Housing and Urban Development 451 Seventh Street, S. W. Washington, D. C. 20410			13. Type of Report and Period Covered Final
			14. Sponsoring Agency Code
15. Supplementary Notes * (A) 0502.01; (B) 0503.02; (C) 1002.01; (D) 1102.01; (E) 0404.04			
16. Abstracts A. Housing Problem Definition (Housing Assistance Plan). This is a free-standing HAP for Huntingdon County. B. Areawide Housing Opportunity Plan (AHOP). This County AHOP was included in Regional AHOP for Southern Alleghenies Region. C. Service Level Analysis - Financial Analysis of Huntingdon County in the past and projections to 1986 as first step in the development of a capital improvements program. D. Energy Legislation and Programs - Analysis of current energy legislation and listing of available funding programs for energy conservation. E. Land Development Alternatives - Redesign of two subdivisions to show good development practices vs. bad development practices.			
17. Key Words and Document Analysis. (a). Descriptors			
17b. Identifiers/Open-Ended Terms			
17c. COSATI Field/Group			
18. Distribution Statement: Available to the Public From: Huntingdon County Planning Commission Court House Huntingdon, PA 16652			19. Security Class: (This Report) UNCLASSIFIED
			20. Security Class: (This Page) UNCLASSIFIED
			21. No. of Pages: 191
			22. Price: $5.00
FORM CFSTI-35 (4-70)			7/73

Figure 12: Bibliographic Data Sheet

> Maryland. Sales and Use Tax Division. *Maryland Sales and Use Tax Tip Number 11: Agricultural Exemptions*. Baltimore, 1990.

SLR 2.3   Title Length

Excessively long titles can be shortened by the use of ellipses for omitted words (see US 2.3).

> Boston, Mass. *East Boston Capital Fund . . . Neighborhood Improvement Program*. 1979.

SLR 2.4   Language of Title

SLR documents may appear in a language other than English. If this applies to your document, give the title in the foreign language following its rules of capitalization. A note can be added if the language is not obvious to the ordinary user (see SLR 6.2).

> Texas. Department of Health. *Disenteria amibiana*. Austin, 1981.

SLR 2.5   Date in Title

If a date appears as part of the title, include it even if another date is cited as the publication data. The use of both dates will let your reader know that the document was published substantially after the time period covered.

> Alabama. Department of Archives and History. *Alabama Official and Statistical Register 1979*. Montgomery: Skinner Print Co., 1982.

SLR 2.6   Personal Authors

Include personal authors in the title statement, preceding the name with "by," "edited by," "prepared by," "compiled by," etc.

> Hawaii. Department of Land and Natural Resources. *The Kalia Burial Site: Rescue Archaeology in Waikiki* by Earl Neller. Honolulu, 1980.

SLR 2.6a If the document was written by more than three people, simply give the first author listed on the document and cover the others by "et al."or "and others."

> Massachusetts. Division of Employment Security. *Occupational Profile of Selected Manufacturing Industries in Massachusetts 1980* prepared by Richard Subrant et al. Boston, 1981. (Occupation/Industry Research Publication 14).

SLR 2.7 **Contractors as Authors**

Sometimes a government agency will contract with a private group to research a problem. Authorship should then be credited to this organization.

> Southwestern Pennsylvania Regional Planning Commission. *Directions in Housing Policies for Low and Moderate Income Families . . .* prepared by the Institute for Urban Policy and Administration, University of Pittsburgh. Pittsburgh, 1972.

SLR 2.8 **Agency Numbering Systems**

Occasionally an SLR document will have a technical or agency report number printed on the cover, title page, or bibliographic information sheet. If so, include this number in the title statement in parentheses, following any personal authors (see US 2.8).

> Texas. Parks and Wildlife Department. Historic Sites and Restoration Branch. *Archeological Testing, Fanthorp Inn . . . Grimes County, Texas* by R.E. Bumett (PWD 4000-294). Austin, 1981.

SLR 2.9 **Medium**

SLR documents appear in all possible forms, and your reader should be informed if the document you are citing is other than book form (see US 2.9). This is done by placing the information in parentheses after the title, personal authors, and agency number, as applicable.

MAP

> Delaware River Basin Commission. *The Schuylkill River and Outdoor Recreation Area* (maps). West Trenton, N.J., 1983. (A cooperative publication with the Pennsylvania Department of Environmental Resources).

MICROFORM

> Delaware. Department of Natural Resources and Environmental Control. *Mosquito Control in Delaware* (microfiche). Dover, 1989.

SLR 3   EDITION

An SLR document may be revised and reissued (see US 3). You should inform your reader which edition you are using in an edition statement.

SLR 3.1   Edition Statement

The edition statement should follow the title.

> North Carolina. Department of Administration. Division of State Budget and Management. Research and Planning Services. *Profile: North Carolina Counties.* 6th ed. Raleigh, 1987.

SLR 3.1a If the edition is included either as part of the title or in an agency report number, you do not need to repeat the information in a separate edition statement.

> Ozark Regional Commission. *The Consolidation of the Southeast Arkansas Solid Waste Authority: A Final Report.* Little Rock, Ark. 1981.

SLR 3.2   Limited Editions

SLR documents frequently are printed in a very limited quantity. If you are aware of this, inform your reader, since it may affect location of the document.

> Illinois. Commerce Commission. Public Utilities Division. *Operating Statistics of the Telephone*

> *Companies in Illinois, Year Ended Dec. 1991.* Ltd.
> ed. Springfield, 1992.

SLR 3.3 Reprints

It is also possible that an item has been reprinted. This
information should be included in your citation as an edition
statement.

> Pennsylvania. Department of Education. Bureau of Curri-
> culum and Instruction. *Han Hanh Duoc Gap* prepared
> by Bui Tri, Louisette Logan, and Fannette N. Gordon.
> Reprinted 1982. Harrisburg, 1980. (Vietnamese).

SLR 4 IMPRINT

Imprint data include place of publication, publisher, and date
(see US 4).

SLR 4.1 Place of Publication

Publication place can most frequently be found in the mailing
address on a document or in the agency's listing on the title
page. For state and territorial documents assume the place of
publication is the capital unless otherwise indicated. Since the
state's name is in the agency statement, inclusion of the state
in the imprint is superfluous.

> Rhode Island. Department of Economic Development.
> *Rhode Island Basic Economic Statistics 1990/91.* 7th
> ed. Providence, 1991.

SLR 4.1a If a state or territorial document was published in a city other
than the capital, use the name of that city as the imprint
location.

> Iowa. Highway Division. *Report on Traffic Control Plan
> Reviews.* Ames, 1990.

SLR 4.1b For regional documents assume the place of publication is the
city in which the regional organization's headquarters is
located. This information is usually available on the title
page. If the state location is listed in the agency statement, it
can be omitted from the imprint.

> Triad Regional Planning Commission (N.C.). *Housing Restoration in the Central Piedmont Area.* Greensboro, 1976.

SLR 4.1c   For multistate regional organizations, include both the name of the city and the state, since these data are not in the agency statement.

> Delaware River Water Authority. *Watershed Study for Southeast New Jersey* by Thomas Bumett. Philadelphia, Pa., 1983.

SLR 4.1d   For local documents you can usually assume the item was printed in the issuing community and, since these data are in the agency statement, they can be omitted from the imprint. If the item was printed elsewhere, give that place in the imprint.

PRINTED IN COMMUNITY

> Richmond, Va. Mayor's Office. *Budget for 1992.* 1991.

PRINTED ELSEWHERE

> St. Paul, Minn. *Community Development Block Grant Funds: Program Years 1975-78.* Minneapolis, 1979.

SLR 4.2   Publisher

State and local governments, as well as regional organizations, usually do not have official publishers and, therefore, contract with various printers. Unless a specific private firm is mentioned, the printer can be omitted from a citation.

NO PRINTER LISTED

> Colorado. Bureau of Investigation. *Crime in Colorado: Uniform Crime Report.* Denver, 1990.

PRIVATE PRINTER

> Louisiana. Secretary of State. *Report of the Secretary of State . . . Jan. 1, 1979-Dec. 31, 1980.* Baton Rouge: Moran Industries, 1981.

SLR 4.3   Date of Publication

The date of publication on SLR documents can usually be found on the title page, in the preface, or in a letter of transmittal at the beginning of the document.

> Maine. State Library. *Libraries in Maine 1990-91.* Augusta, 1991.

SLR 4.3a If no date can be found and the receipt date of the item was stamped on the document, use that date, bracketed, with a "by."

> Rhode Island. Department of Business Regulations. *72nd Annual Report of the Banking Division.* Providence, [by 1979].

SLR 4.3b If you cannot find a date, use "n.d." (no date).

> Illinois. State Board of Elections. *A Candidate's Guide for 1982 Elections.* Springfield, n.d.

SLR 5   SERIES

SLR documents may be part of a series (see US 5). Such documents will have clear series statements on the title or cover pages.

SLR 5.1   Series Name and Number

Include series name and number information in parentheses following the imprint data.

> Alaska. Department of Fish and Game. *Harvest and Use of Fish and Wildlife By Residents of Kake, Alaska* by Anne S. Firman and Robert G. Bosworth. Juneau, 1990. (Technical Paper 145).

SLR 5.2   SLR Documents as Part of a Federal Series

If a document is prepared in cooperation with a federal agency, the report may also have federal agency report numbers (see US 2.8) or be part of a federal document series (see US 5). If this is the case, this fact should be noted in either a title or series statement.

Florida. Department of Environmental Regulation. *Source, Use, and Disposition of Water in Florida, 1980* by Stanley Leach et al. Tallahassee, 1983. (U.S. Geological Survey. Water Resources Investigation 82-4090).

SLR 6 NOTES

For SLR documents the notes section of a citation may be optional or required, depending on the information to be included (see US 6).

SLR 6.1 Required Notes

Required notes are those which would denote loose-leaf format, inclusion in a microform collection (see US 8.30), or mimeographed material.

LOOSE-LEAF

"Reducing, Suspending, or Cancelling Food Stamp Benefits" (Sect. 543, 9 Mar. 1981). In Pennsylvania Department of Public Welfare. Office of Family Assistance. *Public Assistance Eligibility Manual.* Harrisburg. (Loose-leaf).

MICROFORM COLLECTION NUMBERS (see also SLR 8.10)

District of Columbia. Department of Employment Services. *Women in the Labor Force, Washington D.C. and Metropolitan Area 1989.* Washington, [by 1981]. (1991 SRI microfiche S1527-2).

MIMEOGRAPHED MATERIAL

Madison, Wis. Comptroller. *Financial Statements: Auditor's Report for the Year Ended Dec. 31, 1978.* 1979. (Mimeo).

SLR 6.2 Optional Notes

Optional notes are items covering cooperative publishing, language, map scale, or publication type (see US 6.2).

COOPERATIVE AUTHORSHIP

> Oklahoma. Department of Agriculture. Crop and Livestock Reporting Service. *Oklahoma Agricultural Statistics 1981*. Oklahoma City, 1982. (Produced as a cooperative effort with the U.S. Dept. of Agriculture).

LANGUAGE

> Texas. Department of Human Resources. *Chido en hogar de día*. Austin, n.d. (Spanish).

MAP SCALE

> Alaska. Division of Geological and Geophysical Surveys. *Geologic and Materials Maps of the Anchorage C-7SE Quadrangle* by C. L. Daniels (map). Juneau, 1981. (1:2400).

PUBLICATION TYPE

> Pennsylvania. Department of Community Affairs. *Financing Parks and Recreation Facilities in Pennsylvania*. 4th ed. Harrisburg, 1992. (Pamphlet).

SLR 7 **CITING PARTS: ARTICLES, CHAPTERS, AND LOOSE-LEAFS**

If you have a periodical article or a chapter in a document issued by a state, territorial, local, or regional government, you have different citation elements to consider.

SLR 7.1 **Periodicals**

In a periodical citation you must include the personal author, the article's title, the title of the periodical, volume, issue number, date, pagination, and source of the periodical. It is very important that a source note be included to alert your reader to the fact that the item is a government document (see US 7.1).

> Jones, Marie. "Postwar Baby Boom Shifts 80s Labor Supply," *Prairie Employer Review* 3:11 (Nov. 81) p. 1. (Publication of the North Dakota Job Service).

SLR 7.1a If there is more than one author, use the rules outlined in US 7.1b.

SLR 7.lb If there is no personal author, begin the citation with the title of the article.

> "Former College Will Become State's Newest Prison," *Correctional Newsfront* 17:1 (Winter 1991) p. 1. (Publication of the Pennsylvania Department of Corrections).

SLR 7.2 Non-periodicals

If you have a part of a document to cite, the process is slightly different (see US 7.2). Include the author/title of the part being cited, as applicable; pagination for the part; and citation to the item as a whole.

> "The Ferguson Township Comprehensive Plan," pp. 201-219. In Centre Regional Planning Commission (Pa.). *The Planning Document*. State College, 1991.

SLR 7.3 Loose-leafs

A citation to an SLR loose-leaf publication requires the same elements as any loose-leaf document (see US 7.3).

> "Chapter 5-1300: Fire Exits" (Supp. 4, 1975). In Philadelphia, Pa. *Philadelphia Code*. (Loose-leaf).

SLR 8 SPECIAL CASES

Certain SLR documents are so frequently cited, are so well known, or present such unique problems that they are best covered in a separate section.

SLR 8.1 State Blue Books

State "blue books" are government documents which cover various types of information. Usually they provide background data about a state and its government. To cite blue books give the issuing agency; title; personal author, if any; and any relevant imprint data.

> Oklahoma. Department of Libraries. *Directory of Oklahoma: State Almanac 1989-1990*. Oklahoma City, 1989.

SLR 8.1a Some blue books are not written or published by the state but by a private individual or group. Credit should then be given to the private group or publisher.

> Arizona. Department of State. *Bill Turnbow's 1977-78 Arizona Political Almanac* edited by Mrs. Bill Turnbow. Phoenix, 1977.

SLR 8.2   State Laws

Each state issues volumes containing its laws. A citation to a state law should include the law's name and number, if given; date of passage; the volume number and name of the legal set in which the law can be found; and pagination.

> "An Act Amending the Public School System" (Act 38, 4 May 1990), *90 Laws of Pennsylvania*, p. 164.

SLR 8.2a To cite a law before it appears in final book form, give the name, jurisdiction, and number of the law and its date of passage.

> "An Act Providing for the Preservation of the State Lottery Fund" (Pennsylvania Act No. 1991-36, 14 Aug. 1991).

SLR 8.3   State Regulations

States promulgate regulations to uphold the laws. The citation form will depend on the item in hand. If you have the complete regulations of the state in a bound or loose-leaf format, give the name of the regulation; date of promulgation, if known; title number; the name of the book in hand; and any section numbers. If the item is in loose-leaf format, this should be noted.

> "Heat Pollution" (Aug. 1988), Title 25 *Pennsylvania Code*, Sect. 97.81. (Loose-leaf).

SLR 8.3a If you have a document which lists proposed or enacted regulations and updates the bound or loose-leaf edition, give the name of the regulation, action sought, the name of the volume, volume/issue numbers, date, and pagination.

> "Conservation of Pennsylvania Native Wild Plants,"
> proposed rule to amend 25 Pa. Code Ch. 82, *Pennsylvania Bulletin* (17 Oct. 1992), pp. 5171-5188.

SLR 8.4   Local Ordinances

Local ordinances should be cited in a manner similar to state regulations. Again, the exact elements of the citation will depend on the item in hand. Include those elements that would help locate the ordinance within the larger document. Usually you should have the title and internal report numbers, date, and the title of the volume in which the information can be found.

> "Speed Limits Established" (Chap. 16, Pt. 2, Sect. 12, 12 Aug. 1975), *Code of Ordinances of the Township of Patton* (Pa.). State College: Penns Valley Publishers. (Loose-leaf).

SLR 8.5   Legislative Documents

All state legislative document citations should begin with the name of the state and its legislative body. Further hierarchical breakdowns to chamber, committee, and subcommittee should be included in the author statement.

> Oklahoma. Legislature. House of Representatives. Research Division. *Legislator's Guide to Oklahoma Taxes* edited by Alicia Ramming Emerson. Revised ed. Oklahoma City, 1990.

SLR 8.5a In most states bills introduced in each legislative session are numbered sequentially; consequently, the same numbers are used every year. Therefore, it is necessary to alert your reader in the author statement to the legislative session, if possible. Use the session numbers or years as they appear on the document. If this information is not on the document, the imprint date will have to suffice.

> California. Legislature. Assembly. 1991/92 Regular Session. *AB 2541 Earthquake-Safe Building Construction*. Sacramento, 1992.

SLR 8.5b Some states assign printing or report numbers to legislative documentation. If these numbers are helpful in locating or differentiating among similar items, such as amendments to a bill, they should be included in the title statement as agency numbers. If they are not useful as location devices, they may be omitted. If you are unsure about their value, it is best to include them.

PRINTER'S NUMBER

> Pennsylvania. General Assembly. Session of 1992. *Senate Bill 1806, An Act Regulating the Check Cashing Industry . . .* (Printer's No. 2310). Harrisburg, 1992.

REPORT NUMBER

> California. Legislature. Assembly. Committee on Revenue and Taxation. *Implementation of Proposition 13* by Bob Leland (No. 748). Sacramento, 1979.

SLR 8.5c In many states, legislative documents, particularly hearings, are not printed or distributed by the government. The documents are available only from the stenographic firm which transcribed the session. Should this be the case facing you, include in the imprint the name and location of the stenographic firm so your reader will have a potential source for the document.

> Florida. Legislature. House of Representatives. Select Committee on Reapportionment. Subcommittee on Congressional Redistricting. *Meeting, 8 Mar. 1982.* Tallahassee: Southern Reporting Services, 1982.

SLR 8.6   Statistical Abstracts

Most states produce an annual statistical abstract. Although these documents are usually written by a state agency, sometimes universities or private organizations become involved in the production of the abstract. A citation to such reference sources should give the issuing agency or group, title, edition, and imprint data.

> Delaware. Office of Management, Budget, and Planning. *Dimensions on Delaware: A Statistical Abstract for 1979.* Dover, 1980.

SLR 8.6a A citation to specific data should list the table name, volume, and pagination.

> "Milk Cows on Farms . . . 1970-82," p. 298. In University of North Dakota. Bureau of Business and Economic Research. *North Dakota Statistical Abstract 1983*. 2nd ed. Grand Forks, 1983.

SLR 8.7 State Data Center Publications

State data centers are cooperative enterprises between state governments and the U.S. Bureau of the Census. The goal of these organizations is to distribute census data more efficiently and economically to end users. One method of attaining this goal is to issue special census analyses of computer data for states. The reports should be cited as state reports, including issuing agency, title, report numbers, and imprint data.

> Pennsylvania. State Data Center. *Pennsylvania Municipalities: Population and Per Income Estimates* (PSDC88-19-90). Middletown, 1990.

> Texas. State Data Center. *Final Population and Housing Counts for Texas Cities, Counties, SMSA's*. Austin, 1981.

SLR 8.8 University Publications

In most states there is at least one state university whose operation is supported partially by state funding. Theoretically, any documents produced at these institutions are also state documents. However, in most libraries such reports would not be in a separate document collection, but would rather be cataloged with the main collection. Therefore, the best way to cite these documents is to give credit to the personal author(s) first, followed by title, edition, imprint data, series, and notes.

> Ritchie, Martin W., and David W. Hann. *Equations for Predicting the 5-Year Height Growth of Six Conifer Species in Southwest Oregon*. Corvallis, Ore.: Oregon State University, 1990. (Research Paper 54).

SLR 8.8a Universities occasionally publish documents for state agencies as university press books. This information should be included in the imprint statement.

> North Carolina. Department of Cultural Resources. Division of Archives and History. *The Quest for Progress: The Way We Lived in North Carolina, 1870-1920* by Sydney Nathans. Chapel Hill: University of North Carolina, 1983.

SLR 8.9　Agricultural Experiment and Extension Publications

The U.S. government has established throughout the country cooperative intergovernmental organizations which deal with agriculture and home economics. These agencies are known generally as "ag" extension services and agricultural experiment stations. Any citation to documents produced by these agencies should list the standard citation elements of issuing agency, title, edition, imprint, series, and notes.

> Connecticut. Agricultural Experiment Station. *Quality of Chip Dips* by Lester Hankin, Donald Shields, and J. Gordon Hanna. New Haven, 1981. (Bulletin 794).

SLR 8.9a Many universities serve as agricultural extension services and experiment stations. Citations to publications issued directly from these organizations should cite the university as the issuing agency, with personal authors added in the title statement.

> Montana State University. Cooperative Extension Service. *Farm and Home Security* by Roy Linn. Bozeman, 1982. (Circular 1017).

SLR 8.10　Microform Collections

Some SLR documents have been reprinted by commercial micropublishers. If you are using a document republished in microform, cite the document as if it were in paper form and include the micropublisher information in a note.

> Vermont. Secretary of State. *Primary and General Elections Vermont 1980 Including Presidential Preference Primary* prepared by the Vermont Elections Project. Burlington: University of Vermont

Agricultural Experiment Station, 1981. (1981 SRI microfiche S8115-1).

Philadelphia, Pa. City Planning Commission. *Philadelphia Center City Walking Tour.* 1976. (Urban Documents Microfiche Collection PPA-0227).

SLR 8.11 Clearinghouse Documents

Just as in U.S. technical report documentation, there are cases in which SLR reports are distributed by a national clearinghouse, such as NTIS (see US 8.28). If you know that your document is available through such an entity, include this information in a note.

Pennsylvania. Governor's Justice Commission. *Comprehensive Plan for the Improvement of Criminal Justice in Pennsylvania.* Harrisburg, 1978. (NTIS microfiche PB 284 551).

SLR 8.12 State Freedom of Information Material

Most states have a statute similar to the federal Freedom of Information Act through which citizens can request unpublished state documents. The citation elements for such documents are similar to those for FOIA material: personal author, state, and agency affiliation, if applicable; title or subject; document type; any identifying numbers; date; pagination; agency from which the material was requested; nature of the request; date of request; and date of receipt (see US 8.32).

LaVine, William. Pennsylvania. Department of Environmental Resources. Kepone Levels in Spring Creek. Report and Data Gathered from Last Fish Kill, May 1981. 7 pp. Obtained under the Pa. Open Records Act; requested as "Spring Creek Kepone Levels," June 1981; received Dec. 1981.

4

International/IGO Information Resources

International/IGO documents are the publications and documentation (i.e. working papers) of international/intergovernmental organizations. Not included in this category are publications of non-governmental international organizations or those of national governments. For a discussion on citations to publications of national governments, see Chapter 5.

Unlike U.S. federal documents, there is no universal system of organizing international/IGO documents. Consequently, you should provide as many access points as you reasonably can.

The majority of citations will include the issuing agency, a title, a document number (if given), place of publication, publisher, and date. For some agencies, like the U.N., a document number is a good access point to indexes and collections; for others whose only access is a sales catalog, a title and a date of publication are important access points; for still other agencies, there are no catalogs and no indexes, and thus finding their publications will be a matter of a particular library's way of handling them.

I 1   ISSUING AGENCY

The issuing agency, and not the personal author, should be the first element in a citation to an international document because:

1) many documents do not have personal authors;
2) even when they do, many indexes and catalogs do not use the personal author in their indexing;
3) giving the issuing agency as author immediately signals to your readers that they are looking for an international document (i.e., that they may not find it through the usual library channels).

This looks unorthodox for some citations, but it serves a purpose. In the usual citation form for books (author, title, imprint), the organization's role may be completely ignored.

One case in point is the report of UNESCO's MacBride Commission. It is often cited as:

Many Voices, One World. New York: Unipub, 1980.

This is fine for libraries which have it cataloged. However, it does not allow for any access in those libraries which have chosen to keep it in a separate international documents collection. Therefore, a better citation—one that would allow for a variety of locations—is:

U.N. Educational, Scientific, and Cultural Organization. International Commission for the Study of Communication Problems. *Many Voices, One World.* New York: Unipub, 1980.

I 1.1   Single Issuing Agency

A citation begins with the name, in full, of the organization.

U.N. Centre on Transnational Corporations. *Transnational Banks and the International Debt Crisis* (ST/CTC/96). New York, 1991.

I 1.1a   If more than one level in the hierarchy is given, all should be used, from the largest to the smallest unit.

U.N. Economic and Social Council. Commission on the Status of Women. *The Situation of Palestinian Women* (E/CN.6/1991/9). 13 Dec. 1990. (Mimeo).

I 1.1b   When the agency is not listed on the document, but you know its name from another source, include it in brackets. It may save your reader a lot of work searching for the location of an obscure office.

U.N. Educational, Scientific, and Cultural Organization. [Secretariat. Sector for Programme Support]. *Organization of UNESCO Secretariat Since 1946* (PRS.79/WS/47). Paris, 1979.

I 1.2   Multiple Issuing Agencies

When confronted with a document issued cooperatively by more than one agency, use the agency which seems to dominate (e.g., the organization which published it), and list the other agency in a note (see I 6.1d). You cannot be sure under which agency a library will list it or whether either agency will list it in its catalog.

> U.N. Economic Commission for Latin America and the Caribbean. *Transnational Bank Behaviour and the International Debt Crisis* (LC/G.1553/Rev. 1-P). Santiago, 1989. Estudios e Informes de la Cepal 76). (Joint publication of ECLAC and United Nations Centre on Transnational Corporations).

I 1.3   Abbreviations and Acronyms

Except for the U.N. you should not assume that every reader knows the full title of such common acronyms as UNESCO or WHO. Spell out the name in the issuing agency statement. If the name appears in the title, take it exactly as given.

> Southeast Asian Ministers of Education Organization. *Resource Book on SEAMEO* (SEAMES/SPIP-1/ 1981). Bangkok, 1981.

I 1.4   Language of the Issuing Agency

There are three general rules for deciding which name to use for multilingual organizations:

1) Do not make your own translations. If you must use a language other than the one used in the document in hand, take the name from the *Yearbook of International Organizations* (Appendix B).
2) Use the name in the language you are using for the rest of your bibliography, if such a name exists.
3) Be consistent; use the name in the same language throughout, even if the texts of the documents are in different languages. Using a single form of the issuing agency's name ensures that all publications for the agency will be together in an alphabetically arranged bibliography and will be less confusing to your reader.

IN AN ENGLISH-LANGUAGE BIBLIOGRAPHY

> Organization of American States. General Secretariat. *Report on the Situation of Human Rights in the*

Republic of Guatemala (OEA/Ser. L/V/ 11.61; Doc. 47, rev. 1). Washington, 1983.

THE SAME DOCUMENT IN A SPANISH-LANGUAGE BIBLIOGRAPHY

Organización de los Estados Americanos. Secretaría General. *Report on the Situation of Human Rights in the Republic of Guatemala* (OEA/Ser. L/V/11.61; Doc. 47, rev. 1). Washington, 1983.

I 1.5   Parliamentary Body as Issuing Agency

Many international organizations have bodies which meet regularly. These may be called meetings, assemblies, conferences, and so forth. In citing documents which come from these parliamentary bodies you should give the parent organization, the name of the group and any numerical designator the organization uses, and the date of the meeting as it is given on the document. This may be a year, month, and day or days. As a general rule, it is best to follow the practice of the organization.

International Labour Organization. International Labour Conference, 69th Session, 1983. *Report VII: Social Aspects of Industrialisation*. Geneva, 1983.

I 1.5a   If the document comes from a smaller group within the body, include this group in the citation.

U.N. General Assembly, 47th Session. Special Political Committee. *Summary Record of the 3rd Meeting*, 20 Oct. 1992 (A/SPC/47/Sr.3). Official Record. 22 Oct. 1992.

I 1. 5b   If a city is named as the meeting place, include it. For organizations which meet in different places from year to year, this may be important information in locating the document.

U.N. Educational, Scientific, and Cultural Organization. Intergovernmental Council of the International Programme for the Development of Communication, 13th Session, Paris, 17-24 Feb. 1992. *Final Report*. Paris, 1992.

I 1.5c　　If the group and session number are not explicitly mentioned, but you can deduce them from other data (such as a report number), include them in brackets.

> International Atomic Energy Agency [General Conference, 27th Regular Session]. *The Agency's Budget for 1984* (GC(XXVII)/686). Vienna, 1983.

I 1.5d　　Look at the arrangement of the organization's meetings. If, in order to distinguish one publication from another, you need to include more information about the session, do so. In the following example, it is necessary to give the part number because there are three different volumes for texts adopted in the 34th session.

> Council of Europe. Parliamentary Assembly, 34th Session, 3rd Pt. "Opinion #112 (1983) on the texts adopted at the 17th Session of the Conference of Local & Regional Authorities of Europe," *Texts Adopted by the Assembly.* Strasbourg, 1983.

I 2　　　**TITLE**

Titles of international documents range from the very obvious to the very obscure and even to the non-existent. The following rules are meant to give some guidance when you have conflicting information or when it is not apparent what the title is.

I 2.1　　**Title Page**

If the document has different titles on the title page, the front cover, and the spine, use the title as it is given on the title page.

> Council of Europe. European Committee on Crime Problems. *Aspects of the International Validity of Criminal Judgments.* Strasbourg, 1968.

I 2.1a　　If the document is on microfiche, take the title from the appropriate frame and not from the microfiche header. The form of titles on microfiche headers is dictated by the space available and does not always agree with the title page.

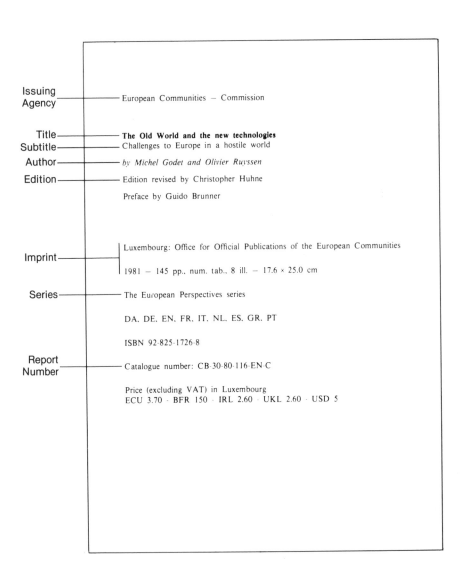

Issuing Agency — European Communities — Commission

Title — **The Old World and the new technologies**
Subtitle — Challenges to Europe in a hostile world
Author — *by Michel Godet and Olivier Ruyssen*
Edition — Edition revised by Christopher Huhne

Preface by Guido Brunner

Imprint — Luxembourg: Office for Official Publications of the European Communities

1981 — 145 pp., num. tab., 8 ill. — 17.6 × 25.0 cm

Series — The European Perspectives series

DA, DE, EN, FR, IT, NL, ES, GR, PT

ISBN 92-825-1726-8

Report Number — Catalogue number: CB-30-80-116-EN-C

Price (excluding VAT) in Luxembourg
ECU 3.70 · BFR 150 · IRL 2.60 · UKL 2.60 · USD 5

Figure 13: CIP Bibliographic Slip

Organisation for Economic Cooperation and Development. *Curtailing Usage of De-icing in Winter Maintenance* (77-89-04-1; microfiche). Paris, 1989.

I 2.1b If the document has Cataloging in Publication (CIP) or a bibliographic data sheet (Fig. 13), use the title as given there.

European Communities. Commission. *The Old World and the New Technologies: Challenges to Europe in a Hostile World* by Michael Godet and Olivier Ruyssen (CB-30-80-116-EN-C). Rev. ed. Luxembourg: Office for Official Publications, 1981. (European Perspectives Series).

I 2.2 Subtitles

Use a subtitle if it will help distinguish common titles or if it will help explain the title's relevance to your research.

International Labour Organisation. *To the Gulf and Back: Studies on the Impact of Asian Labour Migration*. Geneva, 1989.

I 2.3 Title Length

If a title is very long, you need not give the whole title. Do not, however, leave out words in the beginning of the title or any important descriptive words. Omitted parts should be indicated with ellipses (. . .). *Explanatory Report on the Protocol Amending the Convention of 6 May 1963 on the Reduction of Cases of Multiple Nationality and Military Obligations in the Case of Multiple Nationality and Explanatory Report on the Additional Protocol to the Convention of 6 May 1963 on the Reduction of Cases of Multiple Nationality and Military Obligations in Cases of Multiple Nationality* may safely be reduced to:

Council of Europe. *Explanatory Report on the Protocol Amending the Convention of 6 May 1963 on the Reduction of Cases of Multiple Nationality and Military Obligations . . . and . . . on the Additional Protocol. . . .* Strasbourg, 1978.

I 2.4   **Language of Title**

Use the title in the language as given. Do not translate titles even if you give the author and publisher data in your own language (see I 1.4). Use capitalization as shown in the title.

> U.N. Economic Commission for Latin America and the Caribbean. *Reforma agraria y empresas asociativas* (LC/L.497). Santiago, 1988.

I 2.4a   If the publication is multilingual, you do not need to give the title in all the languages listed on the document. Use the title in the language of your bibliography or, if no title is given in that language, use the title in the language you read.

> European Communities. Commission. Statistical Office. *Tax Statistics, 1970-1976* (CA-22-77-613-6A-C). Luxembourg: Office for Official Publications, 1977. (Macroeconomic statistics—purple series).

I 2.5   **Date in Title**

Include dates used in titles and treat them as part of the title. At times the date may be repeated as the publishing date, but frequently the two dates are not the same (see example in I 2.4a).

I 2.5a   For conferences, workshops, and symposia give the place and date after the title but do not underline them.

> Asian Productivity Organization. *Mechanisms and Practices of Agricultural Price Policy in Asia and the Pacific: Report of an APO Study Meeting,* Toyko, 26 Feb.-Mar. 1991. Toyko, 1992.

I 2.6   **Personal Authors**

Although personal authors are not usually mentioned in the documentation of international organizations, many publications (i.e., works created for public sale) do have personal authors. In some libraries sale publications may be treated like other books and may be included in the library's catalog under date and personal author, while in others they may be kept in a separate collection by organization. Because there is no single standard and no way of predicting how such a document will be found, you must be sure both the agency and the personal author's name are given. Place the agency's name first, to conform with other document citations, then the title followed by the personal author.

> U.N. Economic Commission for Europe. *How Partners Spend Their Time: A Comparative Study on Time Use by Men and Women* by Ineke A.L. Stoop and J. Oudhof. Geneva, 1989.

I 2.6a   When there are more than three personal authors, give the name of the first and include the others under "et al." or "and others" (see US 2.6a).

> Organisation for Economic Cooperation and Development. *Japan at Work: Markets, Management and Flexibility* by Ronald Dore et al. (81-89-01-1). Paris, 1989.

I 2.7   **Titles of U.N. Mimeographed Documents**

Titles of U.N. mimeographed documents are often extremely long, confusing in form, and not very informative (Fig.14). Because of this and because the exact title is not very useful in locating U.N. "mimeos," it is permissible to shorten it with ellipses (. . .) or to create a title (in brackets) giving the subject of the document when no meaningful title exists. This is more informative for readers and will not affect their ability to locate the document.

More important is the series/symbol number. It should be included after the title. Other information—place and publisher—may be omitted from citations to the paper copy since it is not given on the document (for citation to the Readex microprint edition see I 2.9). Publication day, month, and year come next. Finally, you should indicate that it is a mimeographed document.

> U.N. General Assembly, 37th Session. *Letter . . . 25 October 1982 from the Permanent Representative of Israel . . . [on the Attack on Credentials of the Israeli Delegation]* (A/37/565). 25 Oct. 1982. (Mimeo).

Publication
Date

Series/
Symbol
Number

Issuing
Agency

Typical
Mimeo
Title

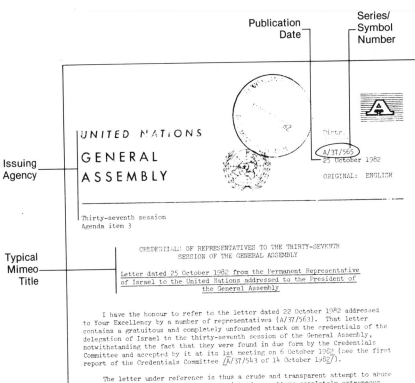

UNITED NATIONS

GENERAL

ASSEMBLY

Distr.

A/37/565
25 October 1982

ORIGINAL: ENGLISH

Thirty-seventh session
Agenda item 3

CREDENTIALS OF REPRESENTATIVES TO THE THIRTY-SEVENTH
SESSION OF THE GENERAL ASSEMBLY

Letter dated 25 October 1982 from the Permanent Representative
of Israel to the United Nations addressed to the President of
the General Assembly

I have the honour to refer to the letter dated 22 October 1982 addressed to Your Excellency by a number of representatives (A/37/563). That letter contains a gratuitous and completely unfounded attack on the credentials of the delegation of Israel to the thirty-seventh session of the General Assembly, notwithstanding the fact that they were found in due form by the Credentials Committee and accepted by it at its 1st meeting on 6 October 1982 (see the first report of the Credentials Committee /A/37/543 of 14 October 1982/).

The letter under reference is thus a crude and transparent attempt to abuse the credentials procedure in order to introduce matters completely extraneous and irrelevant to it. It constitutes one more manifestation of the obsessive hatred towards Israel of certain states which, ever since Israel's establishment in 1948, have been bent on my country's destruction and in the process have flagrantly violated both general international law and the Charter of the United Nations. These violations include most specifically consistent breaches of Article 2, paragraph 4, of the United Nations Charter which prohibits the use and even threat of force against the territorial integrity or political independence of any State, and of Article 2, paragraph 3, of the United Nations Charter which enjoins all members to settle their international disputes by peaceful means.

It is evident that the contentions advanced in the letter under reference would be irrelevant to the credentials procedure even if they were true - which they are not. It is not my intention to be drawn into such abuse of the credentials procedure. I will confine myself to the following observations:

(a) The report of the Credentials Committee is not the occasion for any country to engage in polemics of the kind appearing in the letter under reference;

/...

82-28360

Figure 14: U.N. Mimeo

I 2.8   Organizational Numbering Systems

A few international organizations have devised numbering schemes which they print on some of their documents. Because this number may be useful in some indexes and in some libraries and because each number is unique to a given document, it should be included in parentheses after the title.

Table 3 on the following page shows examples of numbers in the numbering schemes of major IGOs and indicates where on a document the numbers are likely to appear.

Table 3: Organizational Numbering Systems

Organization	Example	Place
United Nations	A/37/565 (see I 2.7)	On mimeo documents in the upper right corner of the first page (see Fig. 14). On *Official Records*, either upper right corner or under title on cover page. On Secretariat (ST/) and other documents may be on back of title page.
European Communities	CA-22-77-613-6A-C (see I 2.4a)	Any or all of the following: back cover, back of title page, bibliographic slip, or cataloging in publication (see I 2.1b) on last page. Often preceded by Kat./ Cat./ (Fig. 13).
Organisation for Economic Cooperation and Development (OECD)	77-89-04-1 (see I 2.1a)	Lower left corner of back cover, small type in parentheses, or last frame of microfiche.
Organization of American States (OAS)	OEA/SER.L/V/11.61 (see I 1.4)	Usually on title page; sometimes also on spine.
Food and Agriculture Organization (FAO)	ADCP/REP/80/11	On title or cover page.
International Atomic Energy Agency (IAEA)		
Documents:	INFCIRC/306	On upper right corner of first page.
Publications:	STI/PUB/498 (see I 7.2)	On back of title page for whole publications.
	IAEA-SM-232/65 (see I 7.2)	On first page of article for individual articles.
United Nations Education, Scientific, and Cultural Organization (UNESCO)	PRS.79/WS/47 (see I. 1.1b)	On lower left or upper right corner of first page; used on documents only, not on UNESCO Press publications.

I 2.9   **Medium**

Like U.S. government documents, international documents come in a variety of media (see US 2.9). You should indicate after the title when the medium is anything other than the traditional book format, unless it is indicated by some other part of the citation.

FILM

> U.N. Centre for Human Settlements (HABITAT). *Action in Rural Living Areas* (film). Nairobi, 1976. (16mm., 15 min., col.).

MAP

> U.N. *A Student Map of the United Nations* (map no. 2753, rev. 4). New York, 1978. (Sales no. E. 78. I. 11).

MICROFICHE

> Organisation for Economic Cooperation and Development. *Household Waste: Separate Collection and Recycling* (97-82-09-1; microfiche). Paris, 1983.

MICROFICHE REPUBLISHED IN COLLECTION

> Nordic Medico-Statistical Committee. *Health Statistics in the Nordic Countries, 1988.* Copenhagen, 1990. (1990 IIS microfiche 2195-51).

MICROFICHE ORIGINAL IN COLLECTION

> International Labour Office. World Employment Programme. *Education and Employment: A Synthesis* by Jan Verslius (WEP 2-18/WP 19). Geneva, 1979. (WEP Research Working Papers in Microfiche 1978).

MICROPRINT (Readex edition)

> U.N. General Assembly, 36th Session. *Preliminary List of the Provisional Agenda of the 36th Regular Session . . .* (A/36/50). 15 Feb. 1981. (1982 Readex microprint).

MIXED MEDIA

> U.N. Educational, Scientific, and Cultural Organization. MAB, Programme on Man and the Biosphere. *Man and the Humid Tropics* by L. Hamilton (slide-tape). Paris: UNESCO Press, 1979. (MAB Audiovisual Series 1).

REALIA (things)

> U.N. [Secretariat]. Office of Public Information. *Flag and Map Kit* (realia). New York, 1976. (Sales no. E/F 76.I.3).

I 3   EDITION

The edition should be cited if there is a likelihood that more than one edition has been issued or will be issued at some time.

I 3.1   Edition Statement

The edition as given on the document should be cited after the title.

> *Everyone's United Nations.* 10th ed. New York: United Nations Department of Public Information, 1986.

I 3.1a   If it is evident from the title or from a report number, the edition need not be cited after the title data.

EDITION AS PART OF TITLE

> Organisation for Economic Cooperation and Development. International Institute for Refrigeration. *Draft Code of Practice for Frozen Fish* (53-69-01-3). Paris, 1969.

EDITION AS PART OF REPORT NUMBER

> European Communities. Commission. *Commission's Proposals to the Council [on] . . . Generalized Tariff Preferences . . . 1982 to 1985 . . .* (COM(81)422 final). Brussels, 1981.

I 3.1b   U.N. Official Records also constitute a final edition of many U.N. mimeographed documents. For instructions on their citations see I 8.2.

I 4   **IMPRINT**

Imprint consists of place of publication, publisher, and date of publication.

I 4.1   **Place of Publication**

Give the name of the place in full (i.e., city and country) unless it is so well-known that it cannot be mistaken.

> U.N. Institute for Namibia. *Toward a Language Policy for Namibia: English as the Official Language, Perspectives and Strategies*. Lusaka, Zambia, 1981. (Namibia Study Series No. 4).

I 4.1a   If the place is not given, write "n.p." (no place). You cannot assume that a document comes from the headquarters city since international organizations have too many branches in too many locations.

> U.N. Economic and Social Commission for Asia and the Pacific. *Handbook on Funding and Training Resources for Disability Related Services in Asia and the Pacific* (ST/ESCAP.541). n.p: United Nations, 1989.

I 4.2   **Publisher**

If the document names a publishing office of the organization, give that.

> European Communities. Commission. *Women and the European Community: Community Action, Comparative National Situations* (CB-24-78-281-EN-C). Luxembourg: Office for Official Publications, 1980.

I 4.2a   When no special publishing agency within the organization is named (as opposed to the Office for Official Publications of the European Communities, for example), assume that the publisher is the organization. Its name need not be repeated.

Council of Europe. European Public Health Committee. *Family Planning.* Strasbourg, 1977.

I 4.2b   If the work comes from UNESCO in Paris and looks like a commercial book (i.e., it has a fancy cover, is typeset rather than photoreproduced from a typescript, and has a title page and a UNESCO copyright), it is probably from UNESCO Press. To distinguish it from other UNESCO publications which are not from UNESCO Press, you should use the Press as the publisher.

U.N. Educational, Scientific, and Cultural Organization. *Biotechnologies in Perspective: Socio-Economic Implications for Developing Countries* edited by Albert Sasson and Vivien Costarini. Paris: UNESCO Press, 1991.

I 4.2c   Some international documents are published for the organization by commercial or university presses.

U.N. Institute for Disarmament Research. *National Security Concepts of States: New Zealand* by Kennedy Graham. New York: Taylor and Francis, 1989.

I 4.2d   When a book is co-published by an organization and a commercial publisher, cite both if the international organization is not named as author.

U.N. Development Programme. *Investing in the Future: Setting Educational Priorities in the Developing World* by Jacques Hallak. Paris: UNESCO International Institute for Educational Planning; Oxford: Pergamon Press, 1990.

I 4.3   **Date of Publication**

The date of publication will usually be found on the title page or on the back of the title page. You need use only the year in most cases.

U.N. Educational, Scientific, and Cultural Organization. Asian Programme of Educational Innovation for Development. *Biology Education in Asia: Report of a*

> *Regional Workshop,* Quezon City, Philippines, 18-23
> Aug. 1980. Bangkok: UNESCO Regional Office for
> Education in Asia and the Pacific, 1980.

I 4.3a If no date is given, but the document has a library date stamp,
write [by year]. This will at least allow your reader to narrow
the search.

> Inter-American Development Bank. *Fifteen Years of
> Activities, 1960-74.* Washington, [by 1976].

I 4.3b If you cannot find any date, write "n.d."

> U.N. Relief and Works Agency for Palestine Refugees in
> the Near East. *Opportunity*, n.p., n.d.

I 4.3c You should omit place and publisher for U.N. mimeos.
However, you must give a complete date. The publication
date can be found under the series/symbol number (Fig. 14).
Ignore other dates for the imprint; they may be used, as
appropriate, in other parts of the citation.

> U.N. Economic and Social Council. *Human Rights
> Questions: Allegations Regarding Infringements of
> Trade Union Right* (E/1992/70). 10 June 1992.
> (Mimeo).

I 5 **SERIES**

A series is a group of publications under one group title with
distinct titles for individual works. They may or may not be
numbered. It is a good idea to include series information in a
citation because:

1) it is often a shortcut in locating the document;
2) if a bibliographic record (index, card catalog, etc.) does not
distinguish individual titles in a series, the series name may
be the only way of locating it.

I 5.1 **Series Name and Number**

Name and number, if applicable, should come in parentheses
after the imprint data.

> U.N. Department of International Social Affairs. *Popula-
> tion Growth and Policies in Mega-Cities: Cairo*

(ST/ESA/SER.R/103). New York, 1990. (Population
Paper No. 34).

I 5.1a   If a document belongs to more than one series, cite all the
applicable series.

> Food and Agriculture Organization of the United Na-
> tions. *Pesticide Residues in Food: Report of the 1976
> Joint Meeting of the FAO Panel of Experts on
> Pesticide Residues and the Environment and the
> WHO Expert Group on Pesticide Residues*, Rome,
> 22-30 Nov. 1976. Rome, 1977. (FAO Food and
> Nutrition Series No. 9; FAO Plant Production and
> Protection Series No. 8; World Health Organization
> Technical Report Series No. 612). (Published jointly
> with WHO).

I 6   NOTES

Some useful information does not fit logically into any of the
previous sections. This kind of information should be placed
in parentheses at the end of the citation. Depending on the
data, notes may be required or optional.

I 6.1   Required Notes

Required notes are those which may help your reader locate
the document.

I 6.1a   Microform collection accession numbers should be given
because such collections are arranged by the accession
number.

IIS MICROFICHE

> International Telecommunications Satellite Organiza-
> tion. *IntelSat Report,* 1990-91. Washington, 1991.
> (1992 IIS microfiche 2090-S1).

FAO DOCUMENTATION MICROFICHE COLLECTION

> Food and Agriculture Organization of the United Na-
> tions. *ESN-Nutritional Country Profile: Barbados*
> (microfiche). Rome, 1989. (FAO acc. no. 290723).

I 6.1b   Include the U.N. sales number in a note when there is no series/symbol number. The sales number may be found on the back cover or on the back of the title page.

> U.N. Department of Public Information. *Basic Facts About the United Nations.* New York, 1987. (U.N. sales no. E. 88.1.3).

I 6.1c   Mimeographed documents should be noted because this will affect your reader's ability to locate them. "Mimeos" are often reproduced only in small quantities and distributed to a few people. It is a good idea to warn your reader that a document may not be in wide circulation. Another category of mimeos comprises U.N. documents which are neither sales publications nor official records. These are not at all difficult to find, but telling your readers that the documents are mimeos will send them directly to an established category of U.N. documentation.

U.N. MIMEOS

> U.N. General Assembly. Preparatory Committee for the United Nations Conference on Environment and Development. *Protection and Management of Land Resources: Compilation of Proposals by Governments, Fourth Session*, New York, 3 Mar.-2 Apr. 1992 (A/CONF.151/PC/105). 15 Jan. 1992. (Mimeo).

OTHER MIMEOS

> Food and Agriculture Organization of the United Nations. Food Preservation Study Group. *Study of Crop Losses in Storage, State of Zacatecas, Mexico 1965-1975* by Hugo Perkins et al. n.p., 1976. (Mimeo).

I 6.1d   If a document is produced jointly by more than one organization, use the most prominent (see I 1.2) as issuing agency/ author and include any others in a note.

> U.N. General Assembly, 45th Session. [Peace Process in El Salvador] *Note Verbale dated 19 October 1990 from the Permanent Representative of El Salvador . . . to the . . . Secretary General* (A/45/667;

S/21906). 24 Oct. 1990. (Mimeo; issued jointly with
the U.N. Security Council, 45th Year).

I 6.2   **Optional Notes**

Optional notes are those which may give your reader a clue
about the nature or characteristics of a document or information which is only marginally useful in locating the document.

I 6.2a   Many international publications destined for sale are given
an International Standard Book Number (ISBN), located
usually on the back cover or the back of the title page. This
number may be helpful in identifying the publication, but it
will not give the average user much help in locating it.
Therefore, its use is optional.

> U.N. Economic Commission for Europe. *Learning and
> the Environment in Europe and North America:
> Annotated Statistics 1992.* New York: United Na-
> tions, 1992. (ISBN 92-1-116537-7).

I 6.2b   Map scale may tell your reader if a map has enough detail.

> European Communities. Commission. *The European
> Community: Member States, Regions and Adminis-
> trative Units* (map). Luxembourg: Office for Official
> Publications, 1981. (1:8000000).

I 6.2c   Film size, running time, and color or black and white may tell
your readers if a film can be used for their purposes.

> U.N. Centre for Human Settlements (HABITAT).
> *Housing in Africa* (film). Nairobi, 1976. (16mm., 15
> min., col.).

I 7   **CITING PARTS: ARTICLES, CHAPTERS, SPEECHES,
PAPERS, LOOSE-LEAFS**

In citing a part of a publication, you must use both the title of
the part and the title of the whole. You would cite a part in a
bibliography when you are referring to a journal article; to an
encyclopedia article; to legal and legislative material in
collections; or to any kind of material published in a collection, such as a yearbook or an almanac.

I 7.1   Periodicals

A periodical citation should include the name of the author, the title of the article, the title of the journal, the volume and issue numbers (if it has these), the date of issue, and the page numbers. It should also include, for U.N. periodicals which have them, the series/symbol number. Finally, unless the periodical is very well known or the organizational source appears in another element of the citation, you should add a note about the issuing organization.

PERIODICAL ARTICLE; PERSONAL AUTHOR; LITTLE-KNOWN JOURNAL

> May, Michael M. "Nuclear Weapons in the New World Order," *Disarmament 15:3* (May 1992) pp. 18-45. (Publication of the United Nations).

PERIODICAL ARTICLE; ORGANIZATIONAL AUTHOR; SERIES/SYMBOL NUMBER

> U.N. Secretariat. Department of International Economic and Social Affairs. Population Division. "Non-governmental Organizations and the World Population Plan of Action," *Population Bulletin of the United Nations* 29 (1990) pp. 54-88. (ST/ESA/ SER.N/29).

PERIODICAL ARTICLE; NO AUTHOR

> "The Community and Events in the Middle East," *Bulletin of the European Communities* 13:9 (1980) pp. 7-8.

I 7.2   Non-periodicals

PAPER IN PROCEEDINGS

> Moghissi, A.A. "Biological Half Life of Tritium in Humans" (IAEA-SM-232/65), pp. 501-507. In International Atomic Energy Agency. *Behavior of Tritium in the Environment: Proceedings of a Symposium*, San Francisco, 16-20 Oct. 1978 (STI/ PUB/498). Vienna, 1979. (Proceedings Series).

ENCYCLOPEDIA ARTICLE

"Abattoirs," pp. 1-3. In *Encyclopedia of Occupational Health and Safety*. 3rd ed. Geneva: International Labour Organisation, 1983.

PAPER IN A COLLECTION

Gao, Fuwen. "The Great Impact of the Educational Satellite System in China," pp. 109-115. In U.N. Outer Space Affairs Division. *Seminars of the United Nations Programme on Space Applications*, 1992 (A/AC.105/492). n.p., 1992.

ARTICLE OR SECTION OF A YEARBOOK

"Children, Youth, and Aging Persons," pp. 809-832. In *Yearbook of the United Nations, 1986*. Boston: Martinus Nijhoff, 1990.

SINGLE CHAPTER WITH PERSONAL AUTHOR

Carrion, Alejandro. "Ecuador," pp. 15-24. In Organization of Petroleum Exporting Countries. Public Information Department. *Not Oil Alone: A Cultural History of OPEC Member Countries*. Vienna, 1981.

SPEECH IN PARLIAMENTARY PROCEEDINGS

Mitterand, Pres. Francois. Speech, 30 Sept. 1982, pp. 291-299. In Council of Europe. Parliamentary Assembly, 34th Ordinary Session. *Official Report of Debates*. Strasbourg, 1982.

I 7.3   Loose-leaf Publications

A few international documents come in loose-leaf format so that they can be easily updated. The date of updating pages, which will usually be found in the top or bottom margin, should be included in the citation. Data about the location of the part within the loose-leaf will depend on the organization of the loose-leaf; it may be expressed in pages, sections, paragraph labels, etc.

"Agreement in the form of an exchange of letters between the European Economic Community and Turkey on imports into the Community of untreated olive oil . . . 1 Nov. 1977 to 31 Oct. 1978" (Sect. Gen. 1, p. 1; 30 June 1979). In European Communities. Council. *Collected Acts: Association Between the European Economic Community and Turkey*, Vol. 2. n.p.: Secretariat of the Council of the European Communities. (Loose-leaf).

I 8   SPECIAL CASES

The citations in this section cover:

1) titles which are so well-known that they do not require as much citation data as other documents;
2) international documents which present unique problems and therefore require special data elements;
3) international documents which are frequently cited and for which this section provides a quick reference.

I 8.1   League of Nations

League of Nations documents fall into two classes: "official publications" and documents which were issued by League agencies, such as the Information Section, but which are not considered official.

I 8.1a   Official documents carry the official publication number, usually in the upper right-hand corner of the title page. It designates to whom the document was distributed, in what sequence, in what year, and in what subject category. Put it after the title in parentheses. This number is used for classification in many League documents collections. You may also find series numbers which you should include in their appropriate place.

> League of Nations. *How To Make the League of Nations Known and To Develop the Spirit of International Cooperation* (C.515.M. 174. 1927.XIIA). Geneva, 1927. (Publications of the League of Nations XIIA Intellectual Cooperation C.I.C.I. 190).

I 8.1b   For some conference documents the official publication number may not be indicated on the document. In that case, give as much information as you can find on the document: dates of the meeting, conference number, sales number (if any).

League of Nations. Conference for the Reduction and
Limitation of Armaments. *Verbatim Record (Revised)
of the 18th Plenary Meeting* . . . 23 July 1932
. . . (Conf.D/PV.18). n.p., 1932. (Sales no.
1932.IX.60).

I 8.1c   If you are citing a League document from a microform
collection, cite the document and then the collection, giving
the location of the document in the collection.

League of Nations. *Protection of Minorities in Poland:
Petition and Annexes*, 23 June 1931 (C.306.1932.IB
and C.306(1).1932.IB). Geneva, 1932. In *League of
Nations Documents, 1919-1946*. New Haven, Conn.:
Research Publications, 1975. (Reel 1B-18).

I 8.1d   When citing an unofficial publication, be as specific as you
can about the issuing agency. You will not find League
numbers (see I 8.1a) on unofficial publications.

League of Nations. Secretariat. *The Aims, Methods and
Activities of the League of Nations*. Rev. ed. Geneva,
1938.

I 8.1e   The League of Nations produced several periodicals over its
existence. Cite these as you would any periodical.

Anigstein, Ludwik. "Malaria and Anophelines in Siam,"
Quarterly Bulletin of the Health Organisation 1:2
(June 1932), pp. 233-308. Geneva: League of
Nations.

Be sure to cite special editions as such.

"The Appeal of the Finnish Government to the League
of Nations," Special Supplement to the *Monthly
Summary of the League of Nations*, December 1939.

I 8.2   **U.N. Official Records**

Three types of U.N. Official Records are issued: supplements,
meeting records, and annexes. Supplements contain reports of
various bodies to the session. Meeting records are verbatim or
summary records. Annexes may contain other material, such

as a list of agenda items. In some sessions there may also be documents not assigned to any of these categories, such as a list of delegations or resolutions and decisions of the Security Council.

I 8.2a   For a supplement, you should cite: the organ and session number, the title and supplement number, the series/symbol number, official record, and the imprint data.

> U.N. General Assembly, 46th Session. *Report of the Human Rights Committee* Supp. No. 40 (A/46/40). Official Record. New York, 1991.

I 8.2b   For a meeting record you should cite: the organ and session number, the subsidiary group (if applicable), the title and meeting date, the series/symbol number, and official record. The imprint data will be limited to the date of publication, usually found under the series/symbol number.

> U.N. General Assembly, 46th Session. Special Political Committee. *Summary Record of the 29th Meeting*, 29 Nov. 1991 (A/SPC/46/SR.29). Official Record. 4 Dec. 1991.

I 8.2c   Annexes usually come in groups. For these you should cite the organ and session number, the agenda item number and title, annexes, official record, and imprint data taken from the title page of the annex (not from the first page of the agenda item number).

> U.N. Economic and Social Council, 55th Session. "Agenda Item 5: The Problem of Mass Poverty and Unemployment in Developing Countries," *Annexes.* Official Record. New York, 1974.

I 8.2d   For documents which do not fall into any of these categories, you should give: the organ and session number, the title and series/symbol (if any), official record, and the imprint data.

> U.N. Security Council, 45th Year. *Resolutions and Decisions of the Security Council 1990* (S/INF/46). Official Record. New York, 1991.

I 8.2e   If any of the above are in microform, be sure to note that fact after the title data for the U.N. edition and in a note for any other.

U.N. MICROFICHE

> U.N. Security Council, 32nd Year. *Resolutions and Decisions of the Security Council 1977* (S/INF/33; microfiche). Official Record. New York, 1978.

READEX MICROPRINT EDITION

> U.N. General Assembly, 37th Session. *Report of the Human Rights Committee* Supp. No. 40 (A/37/40). Official Record. New York, 1982. (Readex microprint).

I 8.3   U.N. Resolutions

The citation for a particular resolution will depend on where you found it, but it should contain enough information to allow your reader to find it in other places. You should include the name and session number (if given) of the organ and the subsidiary body and meeting number (if applicable). The next element is the number, title, and date of the resolution. Not all resolutions have titles. If this is the case with the document you are citing, make up a descriptive title and place it in brackets. From this point the citation will depend on whether you are citing a separate mimeographed document, the official record, or a commercially published collection.

I 8.3a   For a separate mimeo, add the series/symbol number after the title and "mimeo" at the end.

> U.N. Security Council, 2288th Meeting. "Resolution 487 (1981) [On the Israeli Air Attack on Iraqi Nuclear Installations]" (S/Res/487). 19 June 1981. (Mimeo).

I 8.3b   For a resolution in the official records, give the title, series/symbol number, official record, imprint for the official record, and the page numbers.

> U.N. Security Council, 43rd Year. "Resolution 612 [The Situation between Iran and Iraq]" 9 May 1988, p. 10.

In *Resolutions and Decisions of the Security Council* (S/INF/44). Official Record. New York, 1989.

I 8.3c For a resolution from a commercially published collection, add the bibliographic data for the collection.

U.N. General Assembly, 24th Session. "Resolution 2603 Question of Chemical and Bacteriological (Biological) Weapons," 16 Dec. 1969, pp. 226-227. In *United Nations Resolutions, Series I General Assembly*, Vol. XII. Dobbs Ferry, N.Y.: Oceana, 1975.

I 8.3d For resolutions on microform add the medium statement after the series/symbol number for U.N. microfiche or in a note for the Readex microprint.

U.N. MICROFICHE

U.N. Security Council, 2288th Meeting. "Resolution 487 (1981) [On the Israeli Air Attack on Iraqi Nuclear Installations]" (S/Res/487; microfiche). 19 June 1981. (Mimeo).

READEX MICROPRINT EDITION

U.N. Economic and Social Council, 62nd Session. "Resolution 2086 (LXII) Infringements of Trade Union Rights in Southern Africa" (E/Res/2086 (LXII)). 23 May 1977. (Readex microprint).

I 8.4   **U.N. Conferences**

U.N. conference documents will be cited much like other U.N. documents, as official records or as mimeos. The conference, its place, and its date are cited as the issuing agency. If "Official Record" appears as part of the title, it need not be repeated in the edition statement.

MIMEO

U.N. Conference on Desertification, Nairobi, Kenya, 29 Aug.-9 Sept. 1977. *Case Study of Desertification: Mona Reclamation Experimental Project Pakistan* (A/CONF.74/13). n.d. (Mimeo).

OFFICIAL RECORD

> U.N. Conference To Consider Amendments to the Single Convention on Narcotic Drugs, 1961, Geneva, 6-24 Mar. 1972. *Official Records, Vol. I: Preparatory and Organizational Documents; Main Conference Documents; Final Act and Protocol . . . ; Annexes* (E/CONF.63/10). New York, 1974.

I 8.5   **Annual Compendia of the U.N. and U.N. Affiliated Organizations**

The following titles are so well-known that you need cite only the title, date, and imprint data: *Yearbook of the United Nations*; *Statistical Yearbook* (UNESCO); *Demographic Yearbook*.

> *Demographic Yearbook, 1990.* New York: United Nations, 1992.

I 8.6   **U.N. Treaty Series**

Give the parties, the name or type of agreement, the place and date of signing, the U.N. registry number, the name of the series, volume, date, and page numbers.

> Spain and Colombia Agreement on Nationality, signed at Madrid, 27 June 1979 (No. 19299). *United Nations Treaty Series* 1200 (1980) pp. 47-56.

I 8.7   **International Court Reports**

International court reports should all follow the same general form: name of case; type (decision, order, judgment) and date of case; the name and volume of the reporter; and pagination. Some typical examples are given below.

I 8.7a   INTERNATIONAL COURT OF JUSTICE REPORTS

The reports of the International Court of Justice at the Hague are published in two forms—as slip opinions and in bound compilations. The citation is identical for both. The information can be found on the back of the title page.

Continental Shelf (Libyan Arab Jamahiriya/Malta) Order of 26 Apr. 1983, *International Court of Justice Reports 1983*, pp. 3-4.

I 8.7b EUROPEAN COMMUNITIES COURT OF JUSTICE REPORTS

The year on the cover should be used as the volume number; the issue number need not be used since the pagination is continuous throughout the year.

Pierre Favre v. Commission of the European Communities, Order of 7 Feb. 1983 *European Communities Court of Justice Reports 1983*, pp. 199-201.

I 8.7c REPORTS OF THE EUROPEAN COMMISSION AND COURT OF HUMAN RIGHTS

Citations to cases reported in the *Yearbook of the European Convention on Human Rights* should include, after the type of agreement, whose decision (the Commission's or the Court's) is being reported.

Max von Sydow v. Sweden (Decision of the Commission, 12 May 1987), *Yearbook of the European Convention on Human Rights 1987*, pp. 55-72.

I 8.7d Citations to cases reported in *Publications of the European Court of Human Rights* present special problems because this publication is not organized like other court reporters. It has two series: judgments and pleadings. The same case may appear in either series a number of times over a number of years. For these reasons you should cite, in addition to the basic elements given under I 8.7, the series and the imprint data. You can omit pages because each volume is devoted to a single case.

Case of Young, James, and Webster (Judgment of 18 Oct. 1982), *Publications of the European Court of Human Rights: Series A: Judgments and Decisions* Vol. 55. Strasbourg: Council of Europe, Registry of the Court, 1983.

I 8.7e   For Series B there will be a range of dates instead of a date of decision. Include this after the series name.

> Sunday Times Case, *Publications of the European Court of Human Rights: Series B: Pleadings, Oral Arguments and Documents (1977-1980)* Vol. 28. Strasbourg: Council of Europe, Registry of the Court, 1982.

I 8.8   **OAS Official Documents (Records)**

To cite official records of the Organization of American States you should give, as applicable: the full name of the issuing body (including the number, date, and place for meeting records); the title and date of the document; its OAS classification number; official record; and the place and year of publication (if known).

> Organization of American States. Inter-American Nuclear Energy Commission, 10th Meeting, 11-15 July 1977, Lima, Peru. *Final Report* (OEA/Ser.C/ VIII. 10). Official Record. Washington, 1977.

I 8.8a   If you are citing an official document in the microfiche collection, you must add the year, the name of the collection, and the microfiche filing number. You can omit "Official Record" as an edition since it will be given as the title of the collection.

> Organization of American States. Ministers of Foreign Affairs, 17th Meeting of Consultation, 21 Sept.1978, Washington, D.C. *Note from the Ambassador . . . of Nicaragua Requesting Distribution of the Note . . . Concerning Document OAS/Ser L/V/II.45 . . . "Report on . . . Human Rights in Nicaragua"* 15 Feb. 1979 (OEA/Ser.F/II.17; Doc.27/19). Washington, n.d. (1979 OAS Official Records microfiche 79-00002).

I 8.9   **Official Journal of the European Communities**

A citation to the *Official Journal* should contain some kind of title for the action. If it is taken exactly as given, it should be surrounded by quotation marks. If it is a composed title, it should be in brackets. You can also shorten a long title with ellipses. Any reasonable form is acceptable; your choice should be governed by the needs of your paper and by the nature of the title being cited. If you take it as given, do not translate or change punctuation or capitalization. Before 1972 there is no official English version; therefore, you will be citing an edition in French or some other official language.

I 8.9a Before 1967 the rest of the citation will be much like a periodical citation with name, volume/issue number, date, and pages.

> "Résolution portant avis du Parlement Européen sur la proposition de directive concernant les problèmes sanitaires dans les échanges de produits à base de viande," *Journal Officiel des Communautés Européennes* 7:109 (9 July 1964) p. 1710.

I 8.9b From 1967 on the *Official Journal* is split into four parts: the C (Communications) series; the L (Legislative) series; the Supplement; and the Annex (debates of the European Parliament). For the first two you should give the L or C issue number after the title; this will signal your reader to look in Part C or Part L.

> "Commission Regulation (EEC) No. 71/80 of 15 Jan. 1980 altering the import levies on products processed from rice or cereal," *Official Journal of the European Communities* L 11 (16 Jan. 1980) pp. 12-13.

I 8.9c In citing the microfiche edition, you should also give the microfiche number.

> Written Question No. 190/76 . . . 21 May 1976 [on Birth Grants], *Official Journal of the European Communities* C 7 (9 Jan. 1978) pp. 1-2. (1978 O.J. microfiche no. 3).

I 8.9d In citing the debates of the European Parliament before 1967, you will find no indication that they are part of the *Official Journal*. Therefore, you should cite the title given on the document.

"Exposé de M. le Président de la Haute Autorité,"
Assemblée Parlementaire Européenne: Débats
3 (mai-juin 1958) pp. 7-16.

I 8.9e   However, if you are using the microfiche edition for those
same years, you can cite the *Official Journal* in the microfiche note.

"Allocution de M. le Président de l'Assemblée,"
Assemblée Parlementaire Européenne: Débats
1 (mars 1958) pp. 30-32. (1958-59 *Journal Officiel:*
Débats microfiche 1).

I 8.9f   From 1967 on, the debates have been issued as an annex to
the *Official Journal*. "Debates" should be cited as a subtitle.

"Organ transplants," *Official Journal of the European*
Communities, Annex: Debates of the European
Parliament 297 (11-15 Apr. 1983) pp. 268-269.

I 8.9g   Citations to the supplement follow the same form as I 8.9f,
except that an S-number is given in place of a volume
number.

"Public Works Contracts," *Official Journal of the*
European Communities, Supp. S 105 (4 June 1983)
pp. 5-6.

I 8.10   European Parliament Working Documents

Cite the title of the individual document (shortened, if
necessary) and cite *Working Documents* as a series with the
document number. Give the full publication date; no other
imprint information is provided.

European Communities. European Parliament. *Report*
Drawn Up . . . on Persons Missing in Argentina. 24
Oct. 1983. (1983-1984 Working Documents No.
902).

I 8.11   European Communities COM-Documents

In citing COM-Documents, give the COM-number as an
agency report number. Otherwise, it follows the standard
form, except that usually no imprint information is given on
the document.

European Communities. Commission. *Financial Situation of the European Communities on 30 June 1981* (COM(81)400). n.p., [by 1981].

I 8.11a In citing the microfiche edition, you should give the microfiche number. You will also generally find more complete bibliographic data in this edition. Look for the information on the microfiche frames, not on the header.

European Communities. Commission. *Proposal for a Council Directive on Procedures for Harmonizing the Programs for the Reduction and Elimination of Pollution . . . from the Titanium Dioxide Industry* (COM(83)189 final; CB-CO 83 058-EN-C). Luxembourg: Office for Official Publications, 1983. (Microfiche EN-83-11).

I 8.12 **Treaties of the European Communities**

There are two classes of treaties of the European Communities: the treaties which established the EC (i.e., the basic law of the EC) and treaties between the EC and other parties.

I 8.12a Establishing treaties should be cited by name, date, and source. It is not necessary to give the parties because it must be assumed that any EC member country has acceded to the treaty.

Treaty Establishing the European Economic Community, signed in Rome on 25 Mar. 1957, *Treaties Establishing the European Communities* (FX-23-77-962-EN-C). 1978 ed. Luxembourg: Office for Official Publications, 1978.

I 8.12b Treaties and agreements with other parties may be found in the *Collected Acts* (see I 7.3) and in other collections. Cite a title composed of the form of agreement and the subject; if none is given on the treaty, create one and enclose it in brackets. The title should be followed by the names of the parties and the date and place of signing or "doing." Finally, you should cite the source.

[Agreement on Trade] between the European Economic Community and the Swiss Confederation, done at

Brussels, 22 July 1972, pp. 18-31. In European Communities. Council. *Collection of the Agreements Concluded by the European Communities, Vol. 3: Bilateral Agreements EEC-Europe* (1958-1975) (RX-23-77-590EN-C). Luxembourg: Office for Official Publications, 1978.

I 8.13   Working Documents of the Parliamentary Assembly of the Council of Europe

The working documents are published both separately and as a collection.

I 8.13a   A citation to the collected working documents should include the number and date of the session and complete imprint information. These will be found on the title page. Since pagination starts over for each document, omit it; the document number is sufficient for location in the volume.

Council of Europe. Parliamentary Assembly, 42th Ordinary Session, 28 Jan.-1 Feb. 1991. "Report on Economic Reform in Central and Eastern Europe" (Doc. 6351), *Documents*. Strasbourg, 1991.

I 8.13b   A separate working document provides less information. You will find only the name of the issuing agency, a title and document number, and the date of publication. Use the day, month, and year. You may abbreviate the month, but do not use a number for it because there is too great a possibility for confusion between the American style (month/day/year) and the European style (day/month/year).

Council of Europe. Parliamentary Assembly. *Report on Craftsmanship* (Doc. 4938). 20 July 1982.

I 8.14   Official Report of Debates of the Parliamentary Assembly of the Council of Europe

For a general debate, you do not need to give the names of the speakers. Begin with the name of the section and the pagination. (You do not need to name the part of the session or the volume number because, although there may be several volumes of debates in the session, the pagination is continuous.) Follow this with a full citation to the *Official Report*.

"Science and Technology," pp. 628-656. In Council of Europe. Parliamentary Assembly, 33rd Ordinary Session. *Official Report of Debates* Vol. III. Strasbourg, 1982.

I 8.15 Orders of the Day; Minutes of Proceedings of the Parliamentary Assembly of the Council of Europe

Give the name of the section and the page numbers followed by a full citation. You must include the part number of the session with the issuing agency data. There will be more than one volume of *Orders* in each session, and the page numbers are not continuous among them. You should also include, after the title, the number and date of the sitting.

"Violence," pp. 63-64. In Council of Europe. Parliamentary Assembly, 34th Ordinary Session, 3rd Pt. *Orders of the Day: Minutes of Proceedings* 28th Sitting, 28 Jan. 1983. Strasbourg, 1982-1983.

I 8.16 Assembly of Western European Union

Western European Union documents are similar in structure to Council of Europe documents. Most official documents are published in a series called *Proceedings* whose volume and name should be included in the citation.

"Consequences of the Invasion of Kuwait: Continuing Operations in the Gulf Region" (Document 1248: 7 Nov. 1990). In Western European Union Assembly. *Proceedings* Vol. III Assembly Documents. Paris: Dec. 1990.

Foreign Government Information Resources

The publishing patterns of foreign (non-U.S.) countries are as varied as the countries themselves. It is impossible to give examples of all the types of publications you will encounter when working with these documents. This chapter is meant only to give representative examples of the type of information that should be included in a citation. For further models for constructing citations, consult other sections of this manual. Often there will be similarities to the publication patterns of U.S., state, and international publications.

In order to make this section useful to the largest number of people, examples were taken primarily from English language publications, but the principles for citing remain the same regardless of language. In only a few cases have foreign language materials been used when it was necessary to illustrate a particular problem in citation. No attempt was made to cite any foreign language materials in non-Roman alphabets or to deal with problems of transliteration.

When working with foreign publications, spend a few minutes looking at the overall publication pattern of the work you will be citing. This will give you a sense of the information you need to include to lead the next person to this source. A few minutes spent at the beginning of your research will save considerable time at the final stages.

The object in constructing your citation is to enable another researcher to retrace your steps and locate the same material you used. To do this with foreign government publications you must, at the very least, clearly indicate that the work is a publication from a foreign government, what agency within the government is responsible for the publication, the title, who published the item, when and where it was published, as well as any series information. When in doubt about what to include in the citation, err on the side of providing more information than may be needed. It is far better to include something that is unnecessary than to leave out a crucial bit of information.

F 1   **ISSUING AGENCY**

As with all government publications the issuing agency is the key to locating the publication. Therefore, the issuing agency, and not the personal author, should be the first element in the bibliography. Use the agency name in full as it appears on the publication.

F 1.1   **Country Name**

The first element in the "agency" name should be the political entity (country, territory, etc). This immediately signals that the publication is from a foreign government. Use the most commonly accepted short form of the name rather than a more formal long name (e.g., Iceland not Republic of Iceland or Mexico rather than United Mexican States). However, be sure to include enough information to clearly distinguish countries with similar names.

> New Zealand. Cabinet Office. *Honours, Titles, Styles, and Procedure in New Zealand* compiled and edited by Phillip P. O'Shea. Wellington: E.C. Keating, 1977.

F 1.1a   **Country Name as Part of the Title of the Agency**

If the country name, or a form of the country name, is the first word in the agency's name, it is not necessary to repeat the country's name as a separate element of the issuing agency.

> Canadian Advisory Council on the Status of Women. *Women and Labour Market Poverty* by Morely Gunderson, Leon Muszynski, with Jennifer Keck. Ottawa: The Council, 1990.

F 1.1b   **Language of the Country Name**

The rules for the language of the country name are similar to the rules for choosing the language for citing an international organization's multilingual publication (see I 1.4).

1) Use the form of country name as it would normally be found in the language you are using for the rest of your bibliography.

IN AN ENGLISH LANGUAGE BIBLIOGRAPHY

Cameroon. Ministry of Information and Culture. Department of Communication. *Cameroon in Brief.* n.p., n.d.

THE SAME PUBLICATION IN A FRENCH LANGUAGE BIBLIOGRAPHY

Cameroun. Ministère de l'Information et de la Culture. Direction de la Communication. *L'essentiel sur le Cameroun.* n.p., n.d.

2) Be consistent. Use the name of the country in the same form throughout the bibliography. If you have a number of documents in various languages all from the same country, choose the form of the name consistent with the primary language of your bibliography, and use this form throughout the bibliography, regardless of the language of the remainder of the agency name. This ensures that all publications from the same country are grouped together in your bibliography.

3) If the name of the country has changed over time, use the form of the name that was in use when the publication was issued. This will be the country name as it appears on the document. An example of such changes would be Rhodesia, now called Zimbabwe.

F 1.2   Issuing Agency

The second element of the citation is the name of the issuing agency. As with all government publications, the agency responsible for the publication is necessary to locate the publication because:

1) Catalogs and indexes for government publications are generally arranged by agency and often do not list personal authors.

2) Those catalogs and indexes which do list personal authors also list agencies.

3) Many documents collections are arranged by agency rather than by subject and, therefore, materials can be more quickly located if the issuing agency is known.

F 1.2a   Single Issuing Agency

Use the form of the agency name as it appears on the document.

> Finland. Ministry of Social Affairs and Health. *Health for All by the Year 2000: The Finnish National Strategy.* Helsinki: 1987.

F 1.2b   Agency Hierarchy

Many readers will be unfamiliar with the structure of another country's government. Identify the agency hierarchy by using the complete form of the agency's name, from the largest to the smallest unit.

> Cyprus. Ministry of Finance. Department of Statistics and Research. *Economic Report, 1989.* n.p.: Printing Office of the Republic of Cyprus, 1991. (General Economic Statistics: Series I. Report 34).

F 1.2c   Multiple Issuing Agencies

If a document was jointly issued by more than one agency, use the agency that published the document or the one which figures most prominently on the title page. If neither agency is more prominent, use the first one listed. List additional agencies as a note (see F 6).

> Canada. Royal Commission on Electoral Reform and Party Financing. *Interest Groups and Elections in Canada* edited by F. Leslie Seidle. (Research Studies, Vol. 2). Toronto: Dundern Press, 1991. (In cooperation with the Canada Communication Group).

F 1.2d   No Issuing Agency Named

Occasionally you will encounter documents in which no agency is mentioned. If the document does not list an agency but you know it from another source (e.g., from a library's catalog), list the agency. Also scan the preface and introductory material for this information.

If no agency at all can be identified use the name of the country alone, followed by the title.

> Hong Kong. *White Paper – The Development of Representative Government: The Way Forward.* Hong Kong: Government Printer, 1988.

F 1.3 Abbreviations and Acronyms in Agency Names

Since a researcher may be unfamiliar with the structure of the government of another country, spell out the full name of the agency; do not use abbreviations.

F 1.4 Language of the Issuing Agency

If possible, keep the issuing agency name in the same language as the name of the country (i.e., the primary language of the bibliography). If the name of the issuing agency is only given in a foreign language use the name of the agency as it appears on the document, regardless of the language of the rest of your citation. Do not translate. This may result in a citation with parts in two languages, but it avoids any problems with translations.

> Italy. Ministero del Lavoro e della Previdenza Sociale. *Social Security and Its Financing, Report '88* by Giuseppe Vitaletti et al. Roma: Fondazione Giacomo Brodolini & Centro Europa Ricerche, [by 1991].

F 1.5 Legislative Bodies as Issuing Agencies

Most countries have some type of "legislative" body as part of their government structure. These may be called congresses, parliaments, assemblies, etc. Indicate the country, name of the parliamentary body and any subsidiary bodies responsible for the work.

1) Follow the country name with the name of the legislative body.
2) Legislative bodies are often composed of more than one chamber. For example, the British Parliament consists of a House of Lords and a House of Commons, while the Australian Parliament consists of a House and Senate. In citing documents from a legislative body clearly indicate if the document originated in a specific chamber.

3) If a document comes from a committee or other subsidiary of a legislative body, the hierarchy should be given in full.

> Canada. Parliament. Senate. Standing Committee on Social Affairs, Science and Technology. *Children and Poverty: Toward a Better Future.* n.p., 1991.

F 1.5a   **Sessions**

As with publications from the United States Congress, it is often helpful to identify a legislative publication in reference to a particular "sitting" of the legislative body. It may be called a session, parliament, congress, assembly, etc. It is especially important when dealing with generic titles such as "proceedings" or "debates." To identify the session, use the date or range of dates. Also include any designation for a numbered sitting of the body, if available.

> Vanuatu. Parliament. Third Parliament, First Ordinary Session, Second Meeting. *Summarized Proceedings, 22-25 May 1989.* n.p., [1989].

F 2   **TITLE**

Unlike books, the title on a government publication is not always obvious. There may be one or several possibilities when choosing a title.

F 2.1   **Location of Title**

When selecting the title of a document, first choose the title given on the title page as the correct title. If there is no title page choose from the cover title, masthead title, or spine title (in that order of preference).

F 2.1a   **Publications in Microformats**

When citing documents that come in microfilm, microfiche, or opaque microcard, take all the bibliographic information from the document. Do not use the information on the microfiche header or film box, since this is often abbreviated to fit into limited space and is usually incomplete.

F 2.2   Subtitles

Use subtitles to help distinguish among generic titles or works with similar titles, or to indicate the publication's relevance to your research.

> Australia. Human Rights and Equal Opportunity Commission. *Racist Violence: Report of the National Inquiry into Racist Violence in Australia.* Canberra: Australian Government Publishing Service, 1991. (Parliamentary Paper No. 100, 1991).

F 2.3   Title Length

In general use the full and complete title. However, if a title is excessively long you may shorten it by using ellipses (. . .) to replace some of the words. Be careful not to delete words near the beginning of the title, words that add significantly to the meaning of the work, or that define the relationship between the work and your research. Enough of the title must be preserved to make the item easily identifiable.

> Great Britain. Department of the Environment. *Sustaining Our Common Future: A Progress Report . . . on Implementing Sustainable Development.* n.p.: The Department, 1989.

F 2.4   Language of Title

Do not attempt to translate titles. Use the title as it appears on the document.

> Dominican Republic. Secretariado Técnico de la Presidencia. Oficina Nacional de Presupuesto. *Presupuesto de ingresos y ley de gastos públicos del gobierno central.* República Dominicana: ONAPRES, 1988. (Capitulo no. 204, Secretaría de Estado de Relaciones Exteriores).

F 2.4a   Multilingual Publications

If a title is bilingual or multilingual, it is not necessary to include reference in all the languages of the work. In choosing the title follow the same rules used in choosing the agency language. Use the title in the predominant language of your bibliography. If the primary language of your bibliography is not one of the languages used in the work, choose a language that you can read or that you feel is readable by many people.

F 2.4b   Capitalization

In general, use the conventions for capitalization that are consistent with the language of the publication. For English language publications this includes capitalizing articles when they are the first word in the title, and all other substantive words in the title. You do not need to capitalize other articles, conjunctions, or prepositions of less than 5 letters.

If you are unfamiliar with the capitalization conventions of a foreign language, use the capitalization as found on the title page.

> Mexico. Consejo Nacional de Población. *Encuesta en la frontera norte a trabajadores indocumentados devueltos por las autoridades de los Estados Unidos de América diciembre de 1984.* Mexico, D.F.: 1986.

F 2.5   Date in Titles

If there is a date in the title of a work, include it in the title segment of the citation, even if it is later repeated in the date of publication. Dates of publication often differ from the year of an annual report or the date of the information in a publication.

> New Zealand. Department of Statistics. *Inter-Industry Study of the New Zealand Economy, 1986-1987.* Wellington: The Department, 1991.

F 2.6   Personal Authors

If an individual is named as the author (or editor, compiler, etc.) of a work, he or she should be given proper credit. Using normal word order, place the name after the title, noting his/her role.

F 2.6a   One to Three Authors

Up to three authors should be listed individually.

United Kingdom. Office of Population Census and
Surveys. *Developing Questions on Ethnicity and
Related Topics for the Census* by Ken Sillitoe.
London: HMSO, 1987. (Occasional Paper 36).

F 2.6b   More than Three Authors

If more than three authors are listed, you should list the first
author and use "et al." or "and others" for the remainder.

Canadian Environmental Assessment Research Council.
*The Integration of Environmental Considerations
into Government Policy* by Francois Bregha et al.
n.p.: The Council, 1990. (Cat. no. En 107-3/19-
1990).

F 2.6c   Contractors as Authors

Government agencies often contract with private companies
to do research on specific topics. Credit should be given to
the companies producing reports.

Canada. External Affairs Canada. *Studies in Canadian
Export Opportunities in the U.S. Market: Telecommunications Equipment* prepared by Peat Marwick
Consulting Group. Ottawa: External Affairs Canada,
1989. (Cat. no. E73-7/74-1988).

F3   EDITION

The edition statement indicates that a work has been revised
from the original or has a special status (e.g., draft edition).
Any edition information found on the publication should be
included in your citation. This includes numbered and dated
editions or words in the title that indicate a special category
for the document.

F 3.1   Numbered and Dated Editions

If an item has a numbered or dated edition statement, this
should be included in your citation immediately following the
title element.

Australia. Department of Trade. *Survey of Major Western Pacific Economies*. 4th ed. Canberra: Australian
Government Publishing Service, 1986.

F 3.2 **Edition Statement**

If the edition is clearly indicated by words in the title, it does not need to be repeated as a separate element in your citation. Some words that indicate an "edition" as part of a title include: "draft," "preliminary," "final," "summary," etc. These are an essential part of the title statement and should always be included, even if they are only present in the subtitle of the document.

> Canada. Royal Commission on the Future of the Toronto Waterfront. *Regeneration – Toronto's Waterfront and the Sustainable City: Final Report*. Ontario: Queen's Printer of Ontario, 1992. (DSS cat. no. Z1-1988/1-1992-E).

F 4 **IMPRINT**

The imprint should include the following: place of publication, publisher, and date of publication. The imprint data may be located in several different places on the document. Check the document thoroughly for this information. Look on the title page, verso (backside) of title page, last page of text, or on the front or back covers of the document.

F 4.1 **Place of Publication**

The place element should consist of the city where the document was published. It is not necessary to include the country name unless the country name is different from the country name used in the issuing body. Use the place name as it appears on the document; do not translate.

> Canadian Advisory Council on the Status of Women. *Women and Poverty*. Ottawa: The Council, 1992.

F 4.1a **No Place Given**

If no place of publication is given, use "n.p." in this portion of the imprint element. Do not guess at a place of publication.

> Canada. External Affairs and International Trade Canada. *Canada and the World Environment*. n.p.: Minister of Supply and Services Canada, 1992.

F 4.2   **Publisher**

The manner in which government documents are published varies from country to country. In some cases they are published by a central governmental publishing agency similar to the U.S. Government Printing Office, while in others they will be published by the government agency or a commercial publisher. Use the form of the publisher's name as it appears on the document. Do not abbreviate the name unless it is abbreviated on the document itself.

> Canada. Federal Provincial Relations Office. *The European Community: A Political Model for Canada?* by Peter M. Leslie. Ottawa: Minister of Supply and Services Canada, 1991. (Cat. no. CP22-35/1991E).

F 4.2a   **The Issuing Agency as Publisher**

If the publisher is the issuing agency you may, if you wish, abbreviate the name or use a phrase such as "The Department," "The Agency," etc.

> Canadian Institute for International Peace and Security. *The Canadian Navy: Options for the Future* by Robert H. Thomas. Ottawa: The Institute, 1992.

F 4.2b   **Language of Publisher**

Use the publisher's name as it appears on the piece. Do not translate.

> Colombia. Office of the President. *Struggle Against Violence and Impunity: A Democratic Commitment.* Bogotá: Imprenta Nacional de Colombia, 1988.

F 4.2c   **No Publisher**

If you can find no publisher listed in the document, do not attempt to guess at the publisher; if there is none listed leave that element blank.

> United Kingdom. Home Office. *The Response to Racial Attacks: Sustaining the Momentum.* n.p., 1991. (Second Report of the Inter-Department Racial Attacks Group).

F 4.3   **Date of Publication**

Include the date of publication in your citation. Generally, you need to use only the year of publication unless the day and month of publication is needed to adequately identify a document.

> Canada. Health and Welfare Canada. *AIDS Information for the Workplace.* Ottawa: Minister of Supply and Services Canada, 1989.

F 4.3a   **Reprinted Works**

REPRINTS OF EARLIER WORKS

The date of reprinting is not a necessary part of the citation unless the document has been reprinted by a different publisher. Include this information immediately after the information using the words "reprinted by . . . " to indicate that you are giving reprint information.

> Colombia. Office of the President. *Policy of the National Government in Defense of the Rights of Indigenous People.* . . . Bogotá: Ministry of Indigenous Affairs, 1989. (Reprinted by Caja and Agraria, Incora, Indevena, 1992).

REPRINTS OF NON-GOVERNMENTAL PUBLICATIONS

Government agencies sometimes reprint articles or other materials that first appeared as commercial publications. In this case you should include a note citing the original document.

> Canada. Health and Welfare Canada. National Clearinghouse on Family Violence. Family Violence Prevention Division. *Child Maltreatment as a Social Problem: The Neglect of Neglect* by Isabel Wolock and Bernard Horowitz. n.p., [by 1990]. (Reprinted from *American Journal of Orthopsychiatry* 54:4 (Oct. 1984) pp. 241-253).

REPRINTS FROM LARGER WORKS

If the material being cited is from a larger work, even if it is from the same agency, the larger work should be noted.

> Canada. Department of External Affairs. *The Canadian Political System* by Eugene A. Forsey. Ottawa: The Department, 1984. (Reprinted from *How Canadians Govern Themselves,* 1982. Canadian Unity Information Office).

F 4.3b **Date Stamps**

It is a common practice in some libraries to stamp documents with the date of receipt. If no other publication date is available, you may use this date in your bibliography. Include this information in brackets preceded by the word "by." This will at least give a future researcher a reference date.

F 4.3c **No Date of Publication**

If no date of publication is given, use "n.d." for no date.

> Malawi. Office of the President. *Statement of Development Policies, 1987-1996.* Zomba: Government Printer, n.d. (with the Department of Economic Planning and Development).

F 5 **SERIES**

Many government publications are released in series. Providing the series title may give an indication of the agency issuing a publication or a general subject that connects all the publications in the series. A series may or may not be numbered. Depending on the cataloging practices of a library, the series title may be a crucial piece of information for locating the document, and it should be included in your citation.

The series name, contained within parentheses, follows the imprint information.

> Canada. Environment Canada. Parks Service. National Historic Sites. *A Tenant's Town: Quebec in the 18th Century* by Yvon Desloges. Ottawa: Supply and Services Canada, 1991. (Studies in Archaeology, Architecture, and History).

F 6   **NOTES**

Some useful information does not fit logically in the other sections discussed. Include this information in parentheses after the imprint and/or after the series statement.

F 6.1   **Required Notes**

The required notes section includes such things as numbers assigned by the government, special formats such as loose-leaf publications, references to microfiche collections, distribution information, cooperative issuing agencies, translator, etc. Also include here the information regarding unpublished materials available only through direct contact with a government agency.

F 6.1a   **Depository Numbering Systems**

Some publications of foreign governments are issued with a classification number assigned by the central depository distribution agency. If a document number is printed on the publication, or if you know the number from a government-issued catalog, include this number in your citation.

> Canada. Treasury Board Secretariat. Administrative Policy Branch. Regulatory Affairs. *How Regulators Regulate*. Ottawa: Minister of Supply and Services Canada, 1992. (BT56-5/1992).

F 6.1b   **Catalog Numbering Systems**

If there is a catalog number that appears to be significant, include this in your citation as well. These are also useful in locating the document in a library's collection.

> Australian Bureau of Statistics. *Transition from Education to Work*. Canberra: Australian Government Publishing Service, 1991. (ABS cat. no. 6227.0).

F 6.1c   **Microform Sets**

Since the documents that are part of a large microform collection may not have separate listings for each title in the library's catalog, knowing that a document is part of a larger microform collection can often be useful in locating the work.

Include information such as dates, entry numbers, etc. as appropriate for locating materials. Two examples are given below.

READEX'S *PARLIAMENTARY PAPERS*—Include year.

United Kingdom. Parliament. House of Commons. *Industrial Development Act 1982: Annual Report* .... London: HMSO, 1991. (House of Commons Paper 593). (Readex British Parliamentary Papers, microfiche, 1990/91).

MICROMEDIA'S *DIRECTORY OF STATISTICS IN CANADA*—Include entry number if this is an access point.

Canada. Royal Canadian Mounted Police. *National Drug Intelligence Estimate, 1989, with Trend Indicators Through 1991.* Ottawa: RCMP Public Affairs Service, 1991. (1992 *Directory of Statistics in Canada,* microfiche, 22279.002).

F 6.2   Optional Notes

Optional notes contain information that might be useful to a researcher, but not essential for identifying the publication. This could include such things as map scales, format of the publication (e.g.,VHS videotape, press release, posters), availability in other languages, etc. Include this in parentheses as the last element of your citation.

FORMAT NOTE

Canada. Indian and Northern Affairs. Quebec Region. *Quebec Indians.* n.p.: Indian Affairs and Northern Development, 1988. (Poster).

TRANSLATIONS—If you feel it would be helpful to another researcher, you may include a note regarding the availability of a publication in other languages.

Canadian Advisory Council on the Status of Women. *We're Here, Listen to Us!: A Survey of Young Women in Canada* by Janelle Holmes and Eliane Leslau

Siverman. Ottawa: The Council, 1992. (DSS Cat. no. LW31-35/92E; issued in French under the title *J'ai des choses à dire, écoutez-moi*).

F 7   CITING PARTS: ARTICLES, CHAPTERS, TABLES, SPEECHES, PAPERS

The object, when citing a part within a larger work, is to clearly identify both the larger work and the specific piece within that work.

F 7.1   Periodicals

When citing an article from a government journal, magazine, newsletter, etc. you must include information on both the specific article being cited and the periodical in which the article can be found. This is one of the few cases in which the issuing agency is NOT the first element of the citation. Begin with information on the article. Include the author(s) name(s), followed by the title of the article (see F 2.6; US 7.1b-7.1c). If there is no author, begin with the title of the article. The title of the article is given in quotations.

> Abejo, Socorro. "Comparative Analysis of Population Age-Sex Distribution from Sample and Complete Enumeration: 1970 and 1980 Census Data," *Journal of Philippine Statistics* 42:1 (1991) pp. 23-25.

F 7.2   Non-periodicals

Generally, with the exception of periodicals, a bibliography cites an entire work and it is left to footnotes to identify a particular page or section that was used. However, there may be occasions when you need to cite a part of a work that is not a periodical article. These citations might be to a particular paper in a conference, one chapter in a book, or specific tables in a statistical compendium.

As with a periodical article, first identify the part and then give specific information about the entire work.

BOOK CHAPTER

> "Arctic: Barometer of Global Change," pp. 15-1–15-28. In Canada. Environment Canada. *The State of Canada's Environment*. Ottawa: Minister of Supply and Services Canada, 1991. (Cat. no. EN21-54/1991/E).

STATISTICAL TABLE—Give citation to table numbers as appropriate.

> "Population Changes," Table 1, p. 12. In Denmark. Danmarks Statistik. *Monthly Review of Statistics*, No. 6, June 1992. Copenhagen: Danmarks Statistik, 1992.

F8   SPECIAL CASES

F 8.1   Translations of Government Documents

If a document has been translated from its original language into another language, give credit to the translator or translating agency in a note.

> Japan. Defense Agency. *Defense of Japan, 1991*. n.p.: Japan Times, Ltd., 1991. (Translated from the original Defense Agency White Paper by Japan Times, Ltd.).

F 8.2   Legislative Publications

The publications of the legislative bodies of foreign countries are as varied as the publications of the United States Congress. While it is impossible to give examples of all the variations in publishing patterns you will encounter, most countries will have some of the following types of publications: debates, bills, reports, papers (often as part of a series issued by the legislative body), committee publications, acts or laws, etc. Below are examples of a few of these publications from various countries. They are only intended to be models, as an individual country's mode of publication may be significantly different.

F 8.2a   Debates

Many legislative bodies keep some record of their debates.

GENERAL DEBATE—In citing a general debate where several members take part, cite the subject of the debate and provide complete information on the work including title (as it appears on the piece), series number, volume number, pages, and date.

> "Liquor Licensing Bill," In Cook Islands. Parliament. 34th Session. *Parliamentary Debates, Official Report (Hansard)* Vol. 6 (22 June 1988) p. 552. Rarotonga: T. Kapi, Government Printer, 1988.

SINGLE SPEAKER—Indicate who is speaking followed by the body in which the speech can be found.

> King, Tom. "Army (Restructuring)," In United Kingdom. Parliament. House of Commons. *Parliamentary Debates, Official Report (Hansard)* 6th Series, Vol. 195 (22 Feb. 1991) pp. 1031-1034. London: HMSO, 1991.

F 8.2b   Bills

Bills are very often numbered on introduction to a country's legislative body. These numbers are retained until a bill becomes law and are often useful in tracking the progress of legislation. As the numbers are often used again in subsequent years, include the year and/or session number as well as the bill number in your citation. With British materials, inclusion of the regnal year is optional. If you choose to include this, it should follow the year and session number in parentheses.

> United Kingdom. Parliament. House of Lords. *Human Fertilization and Embryology Bill, No. 1, 1989/1990 Session*. (Elizabeth II, 1989). London: HMSO, 1989.

F 8.2c   Committee Publications

Like the United States Congress, many legislative bodies have permanent or temporary committees that perform much of the work of the legislature. These committees often issue reports or other documents. When citing these materials indicate the committee that is issuing the document, title of the document, and any series information.

> Australia. House of Representatives. Standing Committee on Aboriginal Affairs. *Our Future Our Selves: Aboriginal and Torres Strait Islander Community Control, Management and Resources.* Canberra: Australian Government Publishing Service, 1990. (Parliamentary Paper No. 137, 1990).

F 8.3   Constitutions

A constitution can be published as a separate publication, within a yearbook or legislative manual, or as part of a commercially produced collection of constitutions. Where you locate the constitution will determine how you cite the material.

F 8.3a   As a Separate Publication

Construct the citation for the whole work as you would for any book citation (see section F 1-F 5). Since constitutions are often amended over time, be sure to include dates, if the document was amended. If necessary examine any prefatory material or notes to determine the dates of amendments. Include this information in brackets following the name if it is taken from anywhere other than the title page.

> Australia. Parliament. *The Constitution of the Commonwealth of Australia, as Altered to 30 June 1987.* Canberra: Australian Government Publishing Service, 1990.

F 8.3b   Subsections of a Constitution

It is possible that you will need to cite a specific part of a constitution, rather than the whole document. Examine the constitution to determine its organization. The format of a constitution varies greatly from country to country. The object in developing your citation is to identify unambiguously the section of the constitution you are citing. Look for designations such as parts, titles, sections, and articles. Determine the hierarchy within the structure and construct your citation using as many pieces of the hierarchy as may be necessary to identify that portion of the document. It is not necessary to use the name of each part or title, unless it seems necessary to clarify your citation.

> Australia. Parliament. *The Constitution of the Common-wealth of Australia, as Altered to 30 June 1987.* Chapter I, Part II, Section 15(a). Canberra: Australian Government Publishing Service, 1990.

F 8.3c   The Constitution as Found in a Larger Work

> Australia. "The Constitution, as Altered to 1 December 1977 . . . ." pp. 592-654. In *Parliamentary Handbook of the Commonwealth of Australia.* 25th ed., 1991. Canberra: Australian Government Publishing Service, 1991.

F 8.3d   Collections of Constitutions

Publishers have issued collections of constitutions from foreign countries. When citing from these collections give information on both the constitution and the collection in your citation.

> Vietnam. "Constitution of the Socialist Republic of Vietnam [as amended through July 15, 1989]." In *Constitutions of the World.* Dobbs Ferry, New York: Oceana Publications, 1992.

F 8.4   Laws

All governments publish laws in one form or another. The two most common arrangements are a chronological printing of laws and an arrangement where laws on similar topics along with amendments are consolidated. Your citation should indicate exactly what source you have used.

F 8.4a   Chronological Printings of Laws

Treat citations to laws in chronological publications in a manner similar to chapters in a book. Include in your citation the title of the law (use a "short" title if it is available), any number that is assigned to the law, volume and pages if applicable, and the name and imprint information for the publication in which you located the law.

> "Children Act 1989." In United Kingdom. *Public General Acts and Measures,* Chapter 41. (Elizabeth II, 1989). London: HMSO, 1989.

If the name of the country and legislative body is evident from the title of the work, you may omit it.

> "Protection of Movable Cultural Heritage Act 1986" (Act No. 11 of 1986). In *Acts of the Parliament of The Commonwealth of Australia Passed During the Year 1986,* Vol. 1, pp. 119-142. Canberra: Australian Government Publishing Service, 1987.

F 8.4b   **Official Codifications**

As with constitutions, examine the overall structure of the work to determine its organization. Look for volume, title, chapter, section, or similar numbers and present this information in hierarchical order.

> "Northwest Territories Act." In *Revised Statutes of Canada, 1985,* Vol. 6, Chapter N-27. Ottawa: Queen's Printer for Canada, 1985.

F 8.4c   **Privately Published Compilations of Laws**

Private publishers often issue compilations of foreign laws. These may be general compilations or have a specific subject focus.

> China. National People's Congress. Standing Committee. Legislative Affairs Commission. *The Laws of the People's Republic of China, 1979-1982.* Beijing: Foreign Languages Press, 1987.

F 8.5   **Regulations**

Regulations are similar to laws in that they are often published in both chronological forms and subject compilations. The rules for citing them are similar to rules for citing laws. Examine the format of the document. Determine the title; use the short title if there is one, and any identifying numbers attached to the regulation.

> "Foreign Investment Review Regulations," *Consolidated Regulations of Canada, 1978.* Vol. 9, Chapter 872, pp. 6397-6412. Ottawa: Queen's Printer for Canada, 1978.

F 8.6   Official Gazettes

A common method used by foreign governments to inform the public of new laws, regulations, and other items of government business is to issue an official gazette. The format of a gazette will vary considerably from country to country. As with other legal documents, look for identifying numbers that should be included in a citation. Include the title (short title if available), volume and part numbers, source, and pagination.

> "Disclosure of Charges (Banks) Regulation," *Canada Gazette*, Part II, 126:12 (June 3, 1992) pp. 2256-2258. (Registration: SOR/92-324).

F 8.6a   Agency Issuing Regulations

The name of an agency issuing a regulation or notice may be included to clarify a citation.

> Canadian Radio-Television and Telecommunications Commission. "Public Notice 1992-54. Private French-Language Television. Preamble to Decisions 1992-544 to 1992-565," *Canada Gazette,* Part I, 126: 34 (August 22, 1992) pp. 2624-2629.

F 8.7   Census Publications

Many countries conduct censuses on a regular schedule to track population changes. You should clearly indicate in your citation that the material being cited is part of the official census and the year of the census. This may or may not be obvious from the title of the work.

> Fiji. Bureau of Statistics. *Report on Fiji: Population Census 1986. V. 3: Economic Characteristics.* Suva: The Parliament, 1988. (Parliamentary Paper No. 46, 1988).

F 8.7a   If the material you are citing is part of an official census but this is not evident from the title, include the information as a note after the imprint information.

> Canada. Statistics Canada. *Mother Tongue: The Nation.* Ottawa: Supply and Services Canada, 1992. (1991 Census; cat. no. 93-313).

F 8.7b   **Microform Collections of Censuses**

If the census you are citing is from a collection of censuses in microform, include the information on the source of the set as a note (see section F 6.1c).

> Ireland. Central Statistical Office. *Census of Population of Ireland, 1981. V. 3, Household Composition and Family Units.* Dublin: Stationary Office, 1985. (Research Publications *International Population Censuses*: Ireland Reel 1, 1981.2-3).

F 8.8   **Treaties**

Treaties are often issued either as separates or as part of a series; include this information as well as the place and date the treaty was signed and came in force.

> Canada. External Affairs and International Trade. *Fisheries: Exchange of Letters Between Canada and the European Economic Community (EEC), Brussels, January 1, 1984, in Force 1 January 1984.* Ottawa: Queen's Printer for Canada, 1989. (Treaty Series 1984, no. 2). (Cat. no. E3-1984/2).

F 8.9   **British "Command Papers"**

Papers in this series generally originate outside of Parliament but are "presented" to Parliament at the "command" of the monarch. They are then issued by Parliament and printed in various "Command Papers" series. Cite the name of the report, series number (if any), and Command paper number.

> United Kingdom. Parliament. *Britain's Army for the 90's.* London: HMSO, 1991. (Command Paper 1595).

F 8.10   Publications of Canadian Parliamentary Committee Materials

COMMITTEE PROCEEDINGS

The proceedings of Canadian Parliamentary Committees are issued over time as a serial publication generally called *Proceedings of the Standing Committee on . . . .* An issue may have a distinctive title for the topic being covered. Give the name of the committee, number and/or name of the proceeding being cited. Give the information on the proceedings as a whole as a series note (Fig. 15).

> Canada. Parliament. Senate. Standing Committee on Foreign Affairs. *Sixth Proceedings on: The Examination of Negotiations for a North American Free Trade Agreement . . . .* Ottawa: Canada Communications Group, 1992. (Proceedings of the Standing Committee . . . . Issue no. 10, 5 May 1992).

COMMITTEE REPORTS

Named reports of Canadian Parliamentary Committees should be cited by the report name, since many libraries will provide access in this manner. If there is information on the issue number from the proceedings of the committee, also include this as a series note.

> Canada. Parliament. House of Commons. Standing Committee on National Health and Welfare. *Booze, Pills, and Dope: Reducing Substance Abuse in Canada: Report of the Standing Committee . . . on Alcohol and Drug Abuse.* Ottawa: Queen's Printer for Canada, 1987. (Minutes of Evidence and Proceedings of the Standing Committee . . . . Issue no. 28, Aug. 4 & 5, Sept.1 & 17, 1987).

F 8.11   Conferences

It is helpful when citing conferences to give the place and date of the meeting in addition to the usual information included in book citations. Include this information immediately after the title, but do not underline or italicize it.

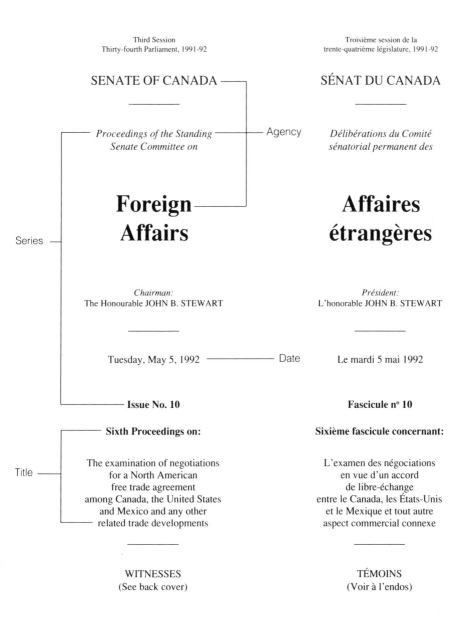

Third Session
Thirty-fourth Parliament, 1991-92

Troisième session de la
trente-quatrième législature, 1991-92

SENATE OF CANADA

SÉNAT DU CANADA

Agency

*Proceedings of the Standing
Senate Committee on*

*Délibérations du Comité
sénatorial permanent des*

Series

**Foreign
Affairs**

**Affaires
étrangères**

Chairman:
The Honourable JOHN B. STEWART

Président:
L'honorable JOHN B. STEWART

Tuesday, May 5, 1992 — Date

Le mardi 5 mai 1992

Issue No. 10

Fascicule n° 10

Sixth Proceedings on:

Sixième fascicule concernant:

Title

The examination of negotiations
for a North American
free trade agreement
among Canada, the United States
and Mexico and any other
related trade developments

L'examen des négociations
en vue d'un accord
de libre-échange
entre le Canada, les États-Unis
et le Mexique et tout autre
aspect commercial connexe

WITNESSES
(See back cover)

TÉMOINS
(Voir à l'endos)

28142

Figure 15: Canadian Parliamentary Material

Canadian Institute for International Peace and Security. *Climate Change, Global Security, and International Governance: Summary of Proceedings . . . .* Ottawa, Canada, 11-12 Apr. 1990 by Kenneth Bush. Ottawa: The Institute, 1990. (Working Paper 23).

F 8.12   Publications of Embassies, Consulates, and Information Agencies

Citations to publications of embassies and information agencies should include the city, state and country (if necessary) in which the embassy or agency is located. Include this information in parentheses following the name of the embassy.

Ireland. Consulate General of Ireland (New York, N.Y.). *Government Statement on the Maguire Case.* New York: The Consulate, 16 June 1991. (Press release).

German Information Center (New York, N.Y.). *Germany's Contribution to the Gulf Effort.* New York: German Information Center, 1991. (Fact sheet).

CHAPTER 6

Electronic Formats of Government Information

An ever-growing amount of information from government sources is available in electronic format. These electronic sources include computer files, CD-ROMs, floppy disks, on-line databases, and electronic bulletin boards (EBBs) distributed by government agencies, as well as products from commercial vendors. These sources contain a wide variety of documents and information, such as numeric data, full-text documents, graphic images, and bibliographic citations. In addition, electronic formats make it possible to duplicate, in whole or in part, an electronic source into a different electronic or paper format.

The combination of different document types, a variety of electronic formats, and a wide range of sources, such as CD-ROMs, on-line databases, electronic bulletin boards, and floppy disks make it important that the researcher provide enough information about the exact electronic source cited to ensure that another researcher can locate this same electronic source. However, providing the information is difficult because many of the sources available in an electronic format may be available in more than one format and must be distinguished from print equivalents or near-equivalents.

The examples in this chapter build upon the basic principles outlined in the preceding chapters and note exceptions and special problems associated with citing electronic resources. The examples are also quite lengthy and contain many different sections. Some are more complete than others because the user may not always be able to locate complete information about an electronic source. **Always provide as much information as you can about an electronic source. The goal is to provide as much information as you can accurately supply that will help the reader locate the exact source cited.**

Punctuation should be used to clarify the relationship between parts of the citation. Citations to electronic sources contain many notes and parenthetical information. If it would clarify and simplify the punctuation of a citation, elements that appear in separate parentheses can be merged into a single set of parentheses and separated by semicolons or other punctuation to make the citation easier to understand and read.

Determining the exact content of a citation is an ever-present problem. Different sources such as the diskette box, the accompanying documentation, and the disk label may give information that does not exactly match, or in the worst instance is contradictory. For this reason it is very important to use the "Internal vs. External" rule for determining which source should be used first.

THE SOURCE OF INFORMATION: THE "INTERNAL vs. EXTERNAL" RULE

Internal sources, such as the item itself, an introductory screen, or an on-disk documentation file (readme or .doc), should be considered the *primary* source of information for electronic format citations. This rule should be used especially when conflicting information is available on an internal source and an external source. External sources, such as print materials accompanying an electronic format (e.g., caddy inserts or user manuals) or a diskette box or envelope, may be lost or misplaced. For this reason, information contained on these sources should be used only to clarify or supplement information contained in an internal source.

Always describe, to the best of your ability, *exactly* what you have in hand or see on the screen to ensure the electronic source is well-identified. Citations to electronic formats tend to be quite lengthy. Don't let the length of a citation deter you from identifying all the parts of an electronic source. Too little information can affect whether a source can be located at a later date.

E 1   ISSUING AGENCY

Government information in electronic format is made available through the efforts of a specific government agency (e.g., through an agency's on-line database or EBB) or is issued by an agency as a product (e.g., floppies, computer files, CD-ROMs). However, electronic formats of government information are also frequently made available by second-party sources (e.g., commercial database vendors, such as DIALOG; non-profit consortia, such as ICPSR; or from regional cooperatives, such as state data centers). Information about these secondary distributors should be included later in the citation (see E 6.1g and E 7.2b).

E 1.1   Single Issuing Agency

If the agency given on the document includes several bureaucratic levels, you should include the name of the country followed by the name of the agency in hierarchical order. Many electronic formats, such as CD-ROMs, include issuing agency information in the form of an agency logo or symbol (Fig. 16). This information should be included, if available.

> U.S. Department of Defense. *Hazardous Materials Information System: HMIS* (DOD 6050.5-L) (CD-ROM). n.p., Feb. 1991. (System requirements: MS-DOS compatible microcomputer, 640KB RAM with 540KB available, CD-ROM drive, *Microsoft Extensions* 2.0 or higher, graphics board, printer; D7.32: Feb. 1991).

> U.S. Department of Health and Human Services. National Center for Chronic Disease Prevention and Health Promotion. *CDP File* (CD-ROM). Atlanta, Ga.: Centers for Disease Control, Apr. 1992. (NCCD-PHP CD-ROM, no. 2). (HE20.7616:2/CD).

Figure 16: Agency Logo/Symbol

E 1.1a   An agency well known in its own right does not need to be preceded by its departmental name.

> U.S. Geological Survey. Earth Science Information Center. *US GeoData (1:2,000,000-Scale Digital Line Graph (DLG) Data)* (CD-ROM). Reston, Va., n.d. (System requirements: IBM PC-XT or compatible, MS-DOS version 3.1 or later, 640KB memory, CD-ROM reader, *Microsoft Extensions* 2.0 or later, EGA display card; I19.120:D56/CD).

E 1.2   **Multiple Issuing Agencies**

If an electronic source has more than one issuing agency, use the first one listed or the one most prominently listed (Fig. 17).

> U.S. Bureau of the Census. *American Housing Survey: 1985N (National) Core & Supplement Tables & Microdata, 1987N Core Tables & Core & Supplement Microdata, 1989N Core Tables, Microdata, Unpublished Tables, 1988, 1989 MSA's Core Microdata* (CD-ROM). Washington: Nov. 1991. (dBase format; C3.214/19:985-89/CD).

**American
Housing Survey**

COMPACT
d i s c
dBASE format

Issued
November 1991

U.S. Department
of Housing and
Urban Development

U.S. Department of Commerce
Bureau of the Census
Data Users Division
Washington, DC 20233
(301) 763-4100

Figure 17: Multiple Issuing Agencies

E 2   **TITLE**

The title of an electronic source can be difficult to determine because there are a wide variety of places this information can be located. However, the title serves as one of the most important parts of the bibliographic citation and care should be taken to identify the exact title for the item in hand or on the computer screen. When absolutely unsure what the title is, take the same title that print indexes (or their computerized equivalents) use (see Appendix B). Exercise caution, however, because electronic formats undergo a variety of title changes and variations over time and the title on the item or on the computer screen may actually help mark it for a specific date and time (Fig. 18 and Fig. 19 show sources of information containing title variations).

> U.S. General Services Administration. *FIRMR/FAR: Federal Information Resources Management Regulation and Bulletins/Federal Acquisition Regulation and Circulars* (CD-ROM). Washington: Government Printing Office, July 1992. (System requirements: IBM PC or compatible, 256KB RAM, DOS 3.1 or later, CD-ROM drive with MS-DOS extensions; GS12.15/2: July 1992).

> Canada. Investment Canada. *The Canadian Edge* (Floppy disk). English software edition for IBM PC and compatibles, Release 3.0. Ottawa: 1988. (System requirements: MS-DOS 2.1 or later, 2MB free hard disk space, 360KB or 720KB floppy disk drive, 512KB memory; accompanied by a user's manual).

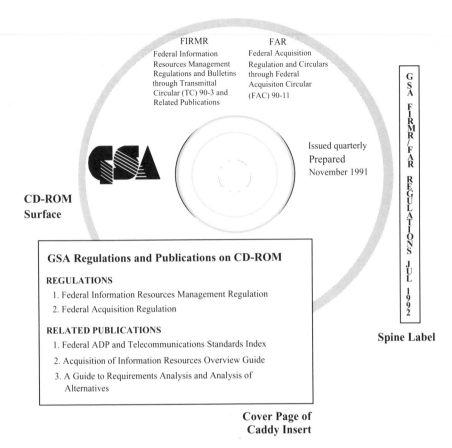

Figure 18: CD-ROM, Caddy Insert, and Spine Label Variations in Title

E 2.1   Subtitles

Frequently electronic formats include a subtitle that further clarifies the content or distinguishes the electronic format from a print or other electronic format version. Such information should be included, separated from the main title by a colon.

> U.S. Coast Guard. *Merchant Marine Examination Questions: Book #4 Deck Safety* (COMDTPUB P16721.25A) (Floppy disk). Washington: Government Printing Office, 1992. (9 disks; system requirements: IBM PC-XT or compatible, MS-DOS; TD5.57/2:4/992/Pt.1).

E 2.2 **Abbreviations in Title**

Use the title as shown, including the use of symbols and acronyms or abbreviations. Provide punctuation when it will clarify the title.

> U.S. Bureau of the Census. *County & City Data Book 1988* (CD-ROM). Washington, May 1989. (C3.134/ 2:C83/1988).
>
> Organisation for Economic Cooperation and Development. *OECD Health Data: A Software Package for the International Comparison of Health Care Systems* (Floppy disk). Paris, 1991. (System requirements: IBM PC or compatible, MS-DOS 3.3 or later, 640KB RAM, hard disk with 4.5MB available and 1 diskette drive; accompanied by: *User's Manual*, 109 pp.).

E 2.3 **Title Length**

In general, the full title included in the electronic format should be included. Frequently this information helps distinguish the electronic version from print or other electronic formats. However, if the title is unusually lengthy and this information does not help distinguish this source from other formats, information may be abridged as shown in US, SLR, I and F 2.3.

E 2.4 **Language of Title**

When a title is provided in two languages, use the title in the primary language of the bibliography (Fig. 19). Add a note to indicate if the text is available in both languages (see E 6.1c).

> Canada. Office of the Auditor General. *Annual Reports, 1981-1991* (CD-ROM). n.p., n.d. (Text available in English or French; includes access software: *OAG*Text*).

CD-ROM Surface

Main Screen

**Cover Page of
Caddy Insert**

Figure 19: Language of Title and Title Variations

E 2.5 Date in Title

Include any dates that are part of the title. Provide punctuation or place the date at the end of the title proper, if it will clarify the information included in the title.

> U.S. Department of Education. National Center for Education Statistics. *NPSAS: National Postsecondary Student Aid Study, 1986-87* (CD-ROM). Washington: Government Printing Office, n.d. (System requirements: IBM PC or compatible, 1MB hard disk space, MS-DOS, CD-ROM player; ED1.333:986-87).

E 2.6 Personal Authors

Personal authors credited with the content of an electronic source should be included in normal word order preceded by the word "by." When more than three authors are listed, list only the first followed by "et al." or "and others."

> U.S. Geological Survey. *Digitized Strong-Motion Accelerograms of North and Central American Earthquakes 1933-1986* by Linda C. Seekins et al. (CD-ROM). n.p., 1992. (Digital Data Series, DDS-7). (ASCII format; system requirements: IBM or compatible, 512KB RAM, MS or PC-DOS 3.1 or later, *Microsoft Extensions* 2.1 or later, CD-ROM drive, hard disk drive; includes access software: *ACATALOG*; I19.121:7).

E 2.7 Agency Numbering Systems

Like print documents, electronic sources will often include a combination of numbers and letters near the title or in the documentation. Since these numbers may be unique to each electronic source, they should be included in parentheses following the title. Do not confuse such numbers with the Superintendent of Documents Numbers (SuDoc) or agency number (see E 6.1h) or the series title and number (see E 5).

> U.S. Nuclear Regulatory Commission. *Licensed Operating Reactors, Status Summary Report, Vol. 6, no. 6* (NUREG-0020) (Floppy disk). Washington, 1992. (Includes access software: *Graybook Report Generator*, April 1991; Y3.N88:15/Vol. 6, no. 6).

E 2.8 Medium

Since many electronic sources are also available in print or in more than one electronic format (e.g., on-line database or CD-ROM), the addition of medium to a citation to an electronic source can be particularly useful. For that reason you should include the medium in parentheses after the title or the report number (if applicable). Since this information is supplied by you to identify the format for the reader, it is recommended that it not be merged into parentheses containing agency report numbers or other title information. Many print finding sources

(see Appendix B) and library catalogs will use the phrase
"machine-readable data file" for all electronic formats. This is
insufficient and it is better to use more specific words or
phrases. The following phrases may be used when appropriate.
However, any phrase that identifies the source format may be
used. Definitions of these terms are included in the Glossary.

CD-ROM	Gopher Server
Computer Tape	Floppy Disk
On-line Database	Electronic Bulletin Board
On-line Database Vendor	Electronic Mail
Software	FTP Site

When a file has been copied onto a computer's hard disk (as
many libraries do), the original format will no longer be
apparent. It may be possible to use external sources (e.g.,
manuals, user aids) to determine the original format. When the
original format cannot be confirmed, use a generic term such as
"machine-readable data file." Some sources will consist of
mixed electronic formats (e.g., floppy disk containing the
software and a CD-ROM containing numeric data). In this
case, use the descriptions that will best help the reader determine that the source is contained in two formats (e.g., software
and CD-ROM).

E 2.8a   You need not include the medium in parentheses when the
information is included as part of the title, series (see E 5.1), or
in a note (see E 6).

> U.S. Occupational Safety and Health Administration.
> *OSHA CD-ROM* (OSHA A92-1). Washington, Oct.
> 1991. (System requirements: IBM PC or compatible,
> 640KB memory, hard disk, MS-DOS 3.3 or higher,
> *Microsoft Extensions* 2.0 or higher, VGA/EGA
> adapter and color monitor, CD-ROM drive; includes
> access software; accompanied by documentation on
> disk; L35.26:92-1).

E 3   **EDITION/VERSION**

Although the words are rarely used, new editions or versions of
documents in electronic formats are frequently issued under a
variety of circumstances, including when data problems are

discovered or when different versions are being tested. While the title, issuing agency, series, etc. will remain the same, the edition information may be the only reliable way to ensure that the title you have cited is not mistaken for another edition of the same title. If you have both an edition, as well as an update, revision, or issue statement, both should be included in the citation.

E 3.1 Edition Statement

Include edition information after the title or report information. When it will clarify, add the word "edition" in brackets.

> U.S. Department of Commerce. Economics and Statistics Administration. *NESE DB: National Economic, Social and Environmental Data Bank* (CD-ROM). Experimental [edition]. Washington, Apr. 1992. (System requirements: IBM PC or compatible, at least 640KB memory, DOS 3.1 or higher, *Microsoft Extensions* 2.0 or later, CD-ROM drive; includes access software: *Browse*; C1.88/2: Apr. 1992).

E 3.1a If the edition is already indicated by the title, you need not repeat it.

> U.S. Bureau of the Census. *Tiger/Line Precensus Files, 1990: New England* (CD-ROM). Washington, Mar. 1990. (dBase format; system requirements: IBM-compatible with 640KB memory, *Microsoft Extensions* 2.0 or greater, can be used with Apple Macintosh computer; accompanied by: *Technical Documentation*; C3.280:N42e/990/CD).

E 4 IMPRINT

Like print and microformat publications, the imprint area should include information that will help alert the reader to a potential source for an item. Some government information in electronic formats can be available from a variety of second-party sources (e.g., a computer-readable file may be available from the agency itself, a commercial vendor, the GPO bulletin board, or a consortium) and in several formats (e.g., on-line database, CD-ROM, and electronic bulletin board [EBB]).

Thus, it is important to use the imprint area to record the actual source you have used for the electronic information you are citing. Many electronic formats include information about the CD-ROM producer or the software developer. This information need not be included in the bibliographic citation unless it is the only information indicating the source of the data.

E 4.1   Place of Publication

The place of publication can usually be found near the issuing agency or a reasonable guess can be made using mailing labels and external sources.

> U.S. Department of Commerce. Bureau of Economic Analysis. Regional Economic Measurement Division. *REIS: Regional Economic Information System* (CD-ROM). Washington, May 1991. (System requirements: IBM PC or compatible, 512KB memory, *Microsoft Extensions*, PC or MS-DOS 3.1 or later, CD-ROM drive; C57.24:991/CD/1).

> United Nations. Statistical Office. *United Nations Women's Indicators and Statistics Microcomputer Database: WISTAT* (Serial no. 001-2.0-01093) (Floppy disk). Version 2. New York, 1991. (Contains 84 data files and 9 reference files in Lotus spreadsheet format, file size ranges from 20KB to 150KB; 7 disks; accompanied by: *User's Guide*, 183 pp.; UN/ST/ESA/WISTAT/ver.2).

E 4.1a   If you can't make a reasonable guess as to the place of publication, use "n.p." (no place).

> U.S. Department of Defense. *HMC&M: Hazardous Material Control & Management/HMIS: Hazardous Material Information System* (CD-ROM). n.p., Feb. 1992. (System requirements: IBM PC or compatible, 640KB RAM, 1MB hard disk space, CD-ROM drive, a graphics board; includes access software; accompanied by: *HMC&M User's Manual*; D212.16: Feb. 1992).

E 4.2 **Publisher**

When a government has a central publishing, printing, or distribution agency (e.g., HMSO or GPO) and that agency is indicated as the source or publisher for the electronic format, include that central agency as the publisher and the agency originating the data or information as the issuing agency (see E 1.1).

> U.S. Energy Information Administration. *U.S. Crude Oil, Natural Gas, and Natural Gas Liquids Reserves, 1977-1990* (DOE/EIA-0216) (Floppy disk). Washington: Government Printing Office, Oct. 1991. (14 files in ASCII format; E3.24:990/floppy).

E 4.2a When an agency is the source of the electronic format, it need not be repeated as the publisher.

> U.S. Geological Survey. *State Water-Data Reports: Hydrologic Records of the United States, Water Years 1990 and 1991* (CD-ROM). n.p, 1992. (Open-File Report 92-478). (System requirements: IBM or compatible, 640KB RAM, MS- or PC-DOS version 3.0 or later, *Microsoft Extensions* 2.1 or later, CD-ROM drive, hard disk drive, color monitor; includes access software: *GSSEARCH*; I19.76:92-478).

E 4.2b When you cannot determine a publisher, simply give the place and date of publication.

> World Bank. *The Education Finance Simulation Model* (Floppy disk). Washington, 1987. (Disk contains file: EDFISIMO.WKS in Lotus spreadsheet format).

E 4.3 **Date of Publication**

The publication or issue date may take the form of a year, a month, or a month or issue date and year (e.g., May 1989; Fall 1992). Be sure to use the form that will ensure that the item can be accurately identified. Do not use software copyright dates as the date of publication for the electronic source itself.

E 4.3a If no publication date can be found in internal or external sources, a date may be supplied using the date included in a library date stamp or based on a reasonable guess (e.g., using the data included). When a date is supplied in this manner, the date should be preceded by the word "by" in brackets.

> U.S. Environmental Protection Agency. Office of Toxic Substances. *Toxic Chemical Release Inventory: Title III-Emergency Planning and Community Right-to-Know Act of 1986* (CD-ROM). Washington, [by 1990]. (2 floppy disks; includes access software: *SearchExpress Retrieval Software*; accompanied by: *CD-ROM Retrieval User Guide*; EP5.22:T65/990).

E 4.3b If you cannot find a date, use "n.d." (no date).

> U.S. Department of Education. National Center for Education Statistics. *High School and Beyond: 1980 to 1986* (CD-ROM). Washington: Government Printing Office, n.d. (ED1.334:980-86/CD).

E 5   **SERIES**

Occasionally an electronic source will be part of a series. These series serve the same purpose they do for print publications—to group distinct titles together. Do not confuse series titles and numbers with agency numbering systems (see E 2.7) or Superintendent of Documents Numbers (SuDoc) or Agency Numbers (see E 6.1h).

E 5.1   **Series Name and Number**

The full series name and the number should come in parentheses after the imprint data.

> U.S. Department of Health and Human Services. National Center for Health Statistics. *National Health Interview Survey, 1987* (CD-ROM). Hyattsville, Md., Dec. 1990. (NCHS CD-ROM Series 10, no. 1). (System requirements: IBM or compatible, 5 MB free hard disk space, DOS 3.0 or higher, *Microsoft Extensions* 2.0 or higher; includes access software: *Statistical Export and Tabulation System (SETS)*; HE 20.6209/4-3:10/1/CD).

E 6   NOTES

Notes can be used to provide information that does not easily fit into any of the categories described above. Notes should provide additional information that will ensure that the reader can identify the exact source cited. They also provide more detailed information about the format of the source and what will be needed to use this source. To help your reader, you should strive to provide as many different notes as possible. **Circumstances may well prohibit you from providing the number and variety of notes shown in these examples; most describe the ideal situation where complete information is available and can easily be determined.** Notes may be grouped at the end of the bibliographic citation in a single set of parentheses; different types of notes can be separated by semicolons.

The different types of notes discussed and shown in Table 4 are in the recommended order for use within the citation. They are listed in the order of their relative importance (from least important to most important) to help the reader identify the exact source cited. Many of the notes help the reader understand what equipment, software, etc. may be needed in order to access or use the electronic source cited. Clearly, this kind of information (data format, system requirements, documentation) will help the reader. However, you may not always be able to provide all or even part of this information. Always include as many notes as you can accurately identify. The Superintendent of Documents Number (SuDoc) or Agency Number should *always* be provided, if known, since these numbers serve as a means of identifying the electronic source in many indexes and library catalogs.

Table 4: Electronic Resources Notes - A Complete List

Data Format (E 6.1a)

Total Number of Disks in a Set (E 6.1b)

Language (E 6.1c)

System Requirements (E 6.1d)

Access Software Included (E 6.1e)

Documentation (E 6.1f)

Clearinghouses and Distribution Agencies (E 6.1g)

Superintendent of Documents Number (SuDoc) or
Agency Number (if known) (E 6.1h)

E 6.1a   Data Format

The format (e.g., ASCII, Lotus spreadsheet, dBase, compressed) of the data should be noted.

> U.S. Energy Information Administration. *CBECS: Commercial Building Energy Consumption Survey, Public Use Data Files, 1989* (Floppy disk). Washington: Government Printing Office, June 1992. (Includes 16 files in ASCII format; 3 disks; system requirements: IBM compatible; includes: *Technical Documentation*; E3.43/2-4:989).

E 6.1b   Total Number of Disks in a Set

Include the total number of original disks. You may not be able to verify the total number of original disks in a set if they have been copied from double-density to high-density disks or installed on a computer workstation. For example, a U.S. government depository library may install the source on a computer with a hard disk. In these cases, the total number of disks could be omitted.

> U.S. Energy Information Administration. *World Energy Projection System (WEPS)* (Floppy disk). Washington, Mar. 1992. (Files in Lotus spreadsheet format; 4 disks; E3.11/20-5:992/floppy).

E 6.1c   Language

When the source in hand or on the computer screen is available in more than one language, include a note indicating the available languages, if known.

> Canada. Statistics Canada. *National Income and Expenditure Accounts: First Quarter 1988* (13-001) (Floppy disk). Evaluation diskette. n.p., 1988. (Text available in English or French; system requirements: IBM PC or compatible with MS DOS 2.0 or higher, one or more 360KB floppy drives, 256KB memory, to view charts an IBM CGA color display adapter and color monitor; includes access software: *Statistics Canada Utility Software*).

E 6.1d   System Requirements

When an electronic source requires specific hardware or software, note these requirements in your citation, if possible. Omission of this information, however, will not limit the reader's ability to locate your document. Typically, this information is found in accompanying documentation or a readme file. Precede this information with the phrase "system requirements:," and use the wording contained in your sources.

> U.S. Energy Information Administration. *PC-AEO Forecasting Model (Annual Energy Outlook;* DOE/EIA-M040 89) (Floppy disk). Version 89C. Washington, 1989. (Lotus spreadsheet format; 3 disks; system requirements: IBM PC or compatible, DOS 3.0 or higher, 1MB RAM, 640K conventional and 768K expanded memory, hard disk drive with 4.5MB free space, *Lotus 1-2-3* 2.01 or higher; accompanied by: *User's Manual*, 50 pp.; available from National Technical Information Service (NTIS), Springfield, Va.; E3.1/5:989).

E 6.1e   Access Software Included

Many electronic sources include access software. Including this information in the citation helps the reader know that this source provides access software. Also, the user may be familiar with the particular software and know that he or she will be better able to access and use the specific source cited. Provide the name of this software and the version, if known. Precede this information with "includes access software:."

> U.S. Department of Commerce. Economics and Statistics Administration. Office of Business Analysis. *NTDB: National Trade Data Bank* (CD-ROM). Washington, Oct. 1992. (2 discs; system requirements: IBM PC or compatible, 512KB memory, CD-ROM drive, *Microsoft Extensions*, DOS 3.1 or later, hard disk, EGA or VGA monitor; includes access software: *Browse* and *ROMWARE*; C1.88:992/3/CD).

E 6.1f   Documentation

When known, the title of print documentation should be noted. Precede the title and total number of pages, if paging is consecutive, with the phrase "accompanied by:." Giving the number of pages helps your reader know how helpful the documentation may be. Many electronic sources include documentation files or directories. When this occurs you may use the phrase "accompanied by documentation on disk."

> U.S. National Center for Biotechnology Information. *Entrez: Sequences* (CD-ROM). Pre-release 6. Washington: Government Printing Office, July 1992. (GenInfo Compact Library Series). (Includes versions for Apple Macintosh and Microsoft *Windows* systems; accompanied by: *User's Guide*, 29 pp.; HE20.3624:992/1/Pre.6/CD).

E 6.1g   Clearinghouses and Distribution Agencies

When clearinghouses or distribution agencies are included as a source (e.g., National Technical Information Service [NTIS]), include that information and location as a note. Include any identification numbers provided.

> U.S. Energy Information Administration. Office of Energy Markets and End Use. *Oil Market Simulation: OMS* (DOE/EIA-MO28(90)) (Floppy disk). Washington, June 1990. (Lotus spreadsheet format; system requirements: *Lotus 1-2-3* version 2; accompanied by: *Demonstration Disk* and *User's Manual*,

> 12 pp.; available from: National Technical Informa-
> tion Service (NTIS), Springfield, Va. (PB89-167886)
> or National Energy Information Center (NEIC),
> Washington; E3.55:990).

E 6.1h   Superintendent of Documents Number (SuDoc) or Agency Number (if known)

U.S. government publications are assigned a classification
number called a Superintendent of Documents Number. This
number is based on the agency providing the electronic source.
It serves as a valuable finding aid in some indexes and catalogs.
Other countries and international and intergovernmental
organizations have similar number systems. When known,
these numbers should be included in the citation.

> U.S. Bureau of the Census. Data User Services Division.
> *U.S. Imports of Merchandise: International Harmo-*
> *nized System Commodity Classification (HTSUSA) by*
> *Country, by Customs District* (CDIM-92-03) (CD-
> ROM). Washington, June 1992 (dBase format;
> C3.278:Im7/June 1992).

E 7   CITING PARTS

Increasingly, electronic bulletin boards (EBBs), CD-ROMs,
floppy disks, and on-line databases provide access to hundreds
of individual databases or files. Thus, it is highly likely that you
will be citing a single periodical article, a single press release,
or a single statistical table that is just *one* of many periodical
articles, press releases, or statistical tables contained in a
database. To complicate the problem, this database may, in
turn, be just one database of many available on an electronic
source, such as an EBB, a commercial vendor's database, a
CD-ROM, or a floppy disk. Thus a citation to an electronic
source can be viewed as having two main pieces: the *electronic*
part and the *electronic source* (see Table 5).

Table 5: The Pieces of a Complete Electronic Citation		
The Electronic Part		**The Electronic Source**
A "Part" of the Electronic Part	The "Whole" Electronic Part	
Include when citing: a single article, statistical table, chapter, court case, press release, code part/section, etc.	Include when citing: an entire periodical issue, data file, book, database, computer file, etc.	ALWAYS include to provide the source for the electronic part being cited.

7.1　The Electronic Part

That piece of the citation that describes the electronic part may be viewed as having two distinct elements:

1) the piece describing the single article, statistical table, chapter, press release, code part/section, or a court case; <u>and</u>
2) the piece describing the whole electronic part containing many articles, statistical tables, an entire book, many press releases, the complete text of the code, or many court cases (see Fig. 20).

The purpose of the citation is to provide the reader with complete information about both pieces (if present), and to clarify the relationship between them. To do so, precede the piece of the citation describing the "whole" electronic part with one of the following phrases:

1) Text from:
2) Data from:
3) Compiled from:

This signals to the reader that all subsequent information refers to the "whole" electronic part you are citing and all preceding information refers to a single piece of this "whole" electronic part. In the electronic part citation include the type of information discussed in E 1-6, paying careful attention to title, author, format, and edition statements, as well as that shown in E 7.1a-7.1c. Although it will be more common to cite a single article, chapter, press release, etc., there may be times when you are citing the whole electronic part. In these circumstances, the first piece of the citation as outlined above is unnecessary.

"PART" OF THE ELECTRONIC PART

Author	Title of "Part"

Gelbard, Robert S. "Security in the America's: Challenges and Opportunities"

Identification No.	Date	Pagination

(File name: V3N445.TXT; 11/18/92; 60032 bytes).

THE "WHOLE" ELECTRONIC PART

Title of Whole	Medium	Date Referenced

Text from: *Dispatch* (On-line database). Referenced: 12/2/92, 3:35p.m. CST

THE ELECTRONIC SOURCE

Name of Source	Medium

Available on: *The Federal Bulletin Board* (Electronic bulletin board).

Vendor Name	Address

Government Printing Office, Washington, 202-512-1397.

Figure 20: Sample Worst Case: Electronic Source

E 7.1a   Identification Numbers or Other Information

Sometimes the best way to identify an electronic part is by a unique identifier, such as a file name or record number in paren-theses after the title. Be sure to include at least one of the following:

1) record identification number and date;
2) exact file name (e.g., 5738102.TXT) and date. Be sure to include <u>all</u> the parts of the file name including the directory, subdirectory, file name extension (e.g., .txt) or menu layers, if they are necessary to locate the exact file cited. Frequently electronic parts must be reached by selecting from a series of menu options, yet the title or file name is not on the first menu selection. When this situation occurs, indicate each menu selection separated by slashes and preceded by the "select menu options" (see example below).
3) in full-text databases, such as a statutes database, individual sections or parts may not have unique identification numbers, other than the statute sections. In these situations, include a complete citation (title, sections, etc.) to ensure that the reader will be able to locate the exact part being cited.

MENU OPTIONS

> "Brazil." (Select menu options: Libraries/Reference Works). Text from: *CIA World Fact Book 1991* (On-line database). Oct. 15, 1991 [edition]. Referenced: 1/2/93, 9:33 a.m., EST. Available on: *Internet Gopher Information Client*, v1.1 (Gopher server). University of Minnesota Computer and Information Services; Internet address: gopher.uiuc.edu.

E 7.1b   **Pagination**

Most electronic sources do not provide page numbers. To help the researcher understand the size of the publication you have cited include at least one of the following in parentheses with the identification number (see E 7.1a), if provided by the electronic source:

1) size of the file (e.g., 2345 bytes);
2) the total number of lines (provided by the database); some systems also express this as "pages"; and
3) an actual page number (when a digitized image of a print source is provided the actual page numbers are usually displayed).

SIZE OF FILE

> "White-Collars Rise as Blue-Collars Decline in Pennsylvania (9/17/92)" (150 lines). Text from: *Bulletins and News Releases* (On-line database). Referenced: 9/28/92, 10:00 a.m. EST. Available on: *EDIN: Economic Development Information Network* (Electronic bulletin board). Pennsylvania State Data Center; Bitnet address: psuvm.

E 7.1c   **Date Referenced (on-line sources only)**

Since the contents of an on-line database can be changed fairly easily and frequently without warning or notice, it is particularly important to record the date and time (including "a.m." or "p.m." and the time zone) the database was referenced. Time is particularly important if a database is updated daily. Precede this information with "referenced:."

"Inventories of Sheets, Pillowcases, and Terry Towels: 1988 to 1992 (Table 1A)." Data from: *Sheets, Pillowcases, Towels, 2nd Quarter, 1992* (On-line database) (File name: IND23X.2QT; 11/12/92). Referenced: 11/30/92, 10:00 a.m. EST. Available on: *Census: BEA Electronic Forum* (Electronic bulletin board). Bureau of the Census, 301-763-7554.

E 7.2 The Electronic Source

The citation must also include a description of the electronic source providing the electronic part. To distinguish between the whole electronic part and the electronic source, precede this part of the citation with the phrase "available on:." This signals to the reader that all subsequent information refers to the electronic source; all preceding information is about the electronic part (see Fig. 20).

The elements of a citation to an electronic source include the information in E 1-6 with the following exceptions:

E 7.2a Issuing Agency

Do not include an issuing agency for electronic bulletin boards or on-line databases. Agencies and commercial sources should be included in the vendor name and address part of the citation (see E 7.2b).

E 7.2b Vendor Name and Address

Do include a vendor name and address for on-line sources, such as EBBs and databases available from a commercial on-line database vendor. This information will help the reader locate or access the electronic source you searched. This address may take the form of an electronic address (Bitnet, Internet, etc.), a city, and/or a direct access phone number.

Gelbard, Robert S. "Security in the Americas: Challenges and Opportunities" (File name:V3N45.TXT; 11/18/92; 60032 bytes). Text from: *Dispatch* (On-line database). Referenced: 12/2/92, 3:35 p.m. CST. Available on: *The Federal Bulletin Board* (Electronic bulletin board). Government Printing Office, Washington, 202-512-1397.

Many on-line electronic sources are now available through a variety of avenues (e.g., on the Internet or via a direct access number). **While readers using your citation may be aware of other avenues to this same source, you are only responsible for documenting the access avenue you used.**

E 7.3   Periodical articles

When citing a periodical article available as part of an electronic source you should provide information about:

1) the author and title of the article (the "part" of the electronic part);
2) the periodical, magazine, or serial title (the whole electronic part); and
3) the electronic source (e.g., EBB, CD-ROM, floppy disk).

Within each of these three sections of the citation it is important to provide as much information as possible as outlined in E 1-E 7.2.

> "Standard Solicitation Documents Available on CD-ROM." Text from: *IRM Newsletter* (Mar. 1992). Available on: U.S. General Services Administration. *FIRMR/FAR: Federal Information Resources Management Regulation and Bulletins/Federal Acquisition Regulation and Circulars* (CD-ROM). Washington: Government Printing Office, July 1992. (System requirements: IBM PC or compatible, 256KB RAM, DOS 3.1 or later, CD-ROM drive with MS-DOS extensions; GS12.15/2: July 1992).

E 7.4   Non-Periodicals

Although many electronic sources are periodicals, many sources are non-periodical in nature, as shown in these examples. Non-periodicals include chapters, statistical tables, press releases, books, speeches, Congressional reports, and entire databases or files.

CHAPTER

"Standard Forms." Text from: *Inventory of Standard and Optional Forms (as of January 31, 1992)*. Available on: U.S. General Services Administration. *FIRMR/ FAR: Federal Information Resources Management Regulation and Bulletins/Federal Acquisition Regulation and Circulars* (CD-ROM). Washington: Government Printing Office, July 1992. (System requirements: IBM PC or compatible, 256KB RAM, DOS 3.1 or later, CD-ROM drive with MS-DOS; GS12.15/2: July 1992).

"Energy: The Atlantic and Western Accords." Available on: Canada. Investment Canada. *The Canadian Edge* (Floppy disk). English software edition for IBM PC and compatibles, Release 3.0. Ottawa, 1988. (System requirements: MS-DOS 2.1 or later, 2MB free hard disk space, 360KB or 720KB floppy disk drive, 512KB memory; accompanied by user's manual).

STATISTICAL TABLE

Many electronic sources include statistical tables. However, frequently the titles or headers for these tables do not provide a sufficient description of the table's contents. For example, the geography (state, county, etc.) or the years included in the table may be omitted from the title. In addition, the order of the information presented in the title or header often reflects the hierarchy of a menu-selection process (state, county, data). When this occurs and when it would clarify the table content to reverse the order of the information, the table title or header may be rearranged. However, in doing so, be sure that the revision includes all important information so that the reader will be able to easily locate the exact data table cited.

"Metal Mining (SIC 1000): Pennsylvania, State Totals, 1988." Available on: U.S. Bureau of the Census. *County Business Patterns, 1988 & 1989* (CD-ROM). Washington, Mar. 1992. (dBase format; includes access software: *CBP*; C3.204/4:1988/89).

PRESS RELEASE

> "NSF Selects RAND to Manage Critical Technologies Institute" (NSF PR 92-64; Aug. 13, 1992; select menu options: Popular FTP Sites via Gopher). Text from: *National Science Foundation Gopher (STIS)* (On-line database). Referenced: 12/17/92, 11:31 a.m. EST. Available on: Internet Gopher Information Client, v1.1 (Gopher Server). University of Minnesota Computer and Information Services; Internet address: gopher.uiuc.edu.

MONOGRAPH OR BOOK

> U.S. International Trade Administration. *A Basic Guide to Exporting, 1992* (ID number: IT Guide; 24 records). Available on: U.S. Department of Commerce. Economics and Statistics Administration. Office of Business Analysis. *NTDB: National Trade Data Bank* (CD-ROM). Washington, Oct. 1992. (CD-ROM Disc 1 of 2; system requirements: IBM PC or compatible, 512KB memory, CD-ROM drive, *Microsoft Extensions*, DOS 3.1 or later, hard disk, EGA or VGA monitor; includes access software: *Browse* and *ROMWARE*; C1.88:992/3/CD).

VOLUME OR PART OF A SET

> U.S. Energy Information Administration. *State Energy Data System 1960-1989, Census Region 3* (DOE/EIA–0214(89)) (Floppy disk). n.p., [by 1991]. (2 Disks; E3.42/5:960-88/Floppy 3).

SPEECH

> "Address by President Delors to the European Parliament Presenting the Commission's Programme for 1990" (Doc. number: 1 17/01/90:Speech/90/1; 1059 lines). Referenced: 1/20/90; 11:15 a.m. EST. Available on: *Rapid* (On-line database). Commission of the European Communities, Brussels.

CONGRESSIONAL REPORT

> U.S. House. *Report [to Accompany H.R. 5983]* (House Report 102-933, (Part)) (577 lines). Text from:

> *Committee Reports* (On-line database). Referenced: 11/23/92, 8:55 p.m. EST. Available on: *LEGI-SLATE*, LEGI-SLATE, Inc., Washington; Internet address: legislate.com.

ENTIRE DATABASE OR FILE

> *Commerce Business Daily* (10 days in file). Referenced 1/3/93, 2:33 p.m., EST. Available on: *EDIN: Economic Development Information Network* (Electronic bulletin board). Pennsylvania State Data Center; Bitnet address: psuvm.

> "MERDB.DTA" (777,962 bytes). Available on: U.S. Energy Information Administration. *Monthly Energy Review Database* (DOE/EIA-0035) (Floppy disk). Washington, Oct. 1991. (ASCII format; E3.9/2:991/10/floppy).

E 8   SPECIAL CASES

Electronic sources are full of special cases because there are so many categories of electronic information and electronic sources, and they are presently in a pattern of constant development and evolution. However, the following titles are those most likely to be encountered.

This section follows the principles outlined in the other chapters, and using the sections in E 1-7 you should be able to modify examples shown in other chapters to accommodate an electronic version of any source. As always, the goals for citations to electronic formats are to be able to distinguish the electronic version from the print equivalent and to provide enough information about the source that the reader will able to locate the same source.

E 8.1   Congressional Record

The *Congressional Record* is published in a bound version and a daily version. The pagination within these two versions differs. Electronic forms of the *Congressional Record* may blur this distinction, as you will see in the following example. However, if provided, it is important to note whether the page number you have included is from the daily or bound version. In addition, when available, also provide the exact day of the *Congressional Record* as well as the volume, and parts (if applicable).

> Sen. Specter (Pa.). "State Visits and Meetings with Foreign Leaders During Recent Recess" (Feb.7, 1990; 1990 WL 23024 Cong.Rec.). Text from: *Congressional Record* (On-line database). Referenced: 12/22/92, 7:05 p.m. EST. Available on: *WESTLAW,* West Publishing Co., St. Paul, Minn.

The Government Printing Office has issued a test CD-ROM of the *Congressional Record.* The following example shows two versions of the same citation for this CD-ROM—a long version and a short version; either is acceptable.

CD-ROM LONG VERSION

> Sen. Pryor (Ark.). "International Youth Year in Arkansas (includes 'Proclamation' by Bill Clinton, Governor of the State of Arkansas)," *Congressional Record*, 131, Pt. 1 (May 15, 1985) bound page: 12182; daily page: S6293 (CD-ROM). Washington, Government Printing Office, 1990. (CD-ROM Disc 1 of 2; system requirements: IBM PC or compatible, 640KB memory, PC- or MS-DOS 3.1 or higher, floppy or hard disk drive, CD-ROM drive, DOS extensions software; includes access software; accompanied by: *Quick Reference Card*, 2 pp. and *Congressional Record on CD-ROM Tutorial and Reference Manual*, 137 pp.; X.99/1:131/CD1).

CD-ROM SHORT VERSION

> Sen. Pryor (Ark.). "International Youth Year in Arkansas (includes 'Proclamation' by Bill Clinton, Governor of the State of Arkansas)," *Congressional Record* 131, Pt. 1 (May 15, 1985) bound page: 12182; daily page: S6293 (CD-ROM). Washington, Government Printing Office, 1990 (X.99/1:131/CD1).

E 8.2   Bills

A bill may go through several versions and an electronic source may provide the text of all or some of these. Thus, it is very important to include the bill version in any citation to a bill, if that information is not included elsewhere in the citation. The Congress number and session are also required for a complete and accurate citation.

> U.S. House. 102nd Congress, 2nd Session. *H.R. 5983, Government Printing Office Electronic Information Access Enhancement Act of 1992*. As passed by the House (engrossed). Text from: *Quick Bill* (On-line database). Referenced: 11/23/92, 8:55 a.m. EST. Available on: *LEGI-SLATE*, LEGI-SLATE, Inc., Washington; Internet address: legislate.com.

BILL TEXT WITHIN ANOTHER SOURCE

In this example, the date of the *Congressional Record* indirectly provides the bill version.

> U.S. House. 102nd Congress, 2nd Session. *H.R. 5983, Government Printing Office Electronic Information Access Enhancement Act of 1992* (103 lines; *Congressional Record*, Sept. 22, 1992, page E2737). Text from: *Congressional Record* (On-line database). Referenced: 11/23/92, 8:57 p.m. EST. Available on: *LEGI-SLATE*, LEGI-SLATE, Inc., Washington; Internet address: legislate.com.

E 8.3 Statutes

Since a jurisdiction's statutes are updated on a regular basis, it is important to let the reader know the date of the text you are citing. Different electronic sources provide this information in different forms. The examples below give some of the forms used most frequently.

U.S. CODE

> "Joint Committee on Printing: Membership" (Title 44 *U.S. Code*, Pt. 102 (as of Dec. 31, 1986); 89 lines). Text from: *Current USC* (On-line database). Referenced: 1/13/92, 2:03 p.m. EST. Available on: *LEGI-SLATE*, LEGI-SLATE, Inc., Washington; Internet address: legislate.com.

"Americans with Disabilities Act: ADA (text as signed by President)" (48810 bytes). Text from: /PUB/ADA/ADA726.ZIP (Computer file). Referenced: 12/15/92, 6:55 p.m., EST. Available from: handicap.shel.isc-br.com (129.189.4.184) (FTP site).

STATE CODE

"Intoxication or Drugged Condition" (Title 18 *Purdon's Pennsylvania Consolidated Statutes Annotated*, Pt. 308 (as amended 1976, Apr. 7, PL 72, no. 32, section 1; 60 pages). Text from: *PA-ST-ANN* (On-line database). Referenced: 6/15/92, 9:35 a.m. EST. Available on: *WESTLAW*, West Publishing Co., St. Paul, Minn.

LEGISLATIVE SERVICE

"Tuition Account Program and College Savings Bond Act," Act 1992-11 (S.B. no. 2; 42 pages). Text from: *PA-LEGIS* (On-line database). Referenced: 12/5/92, 4:30 p.m. EST. Available on: *WESTLAW*, West Publishing Co., St. Paul, Minn.

E 8.4   Federal Register

A citation to the *Federal Register* should allow the reader to find the exact section cited without having to search the entire text of a daily issue. Most systems have developed a unique identifier for each section. This identifier should be included in parentheses immediately following the section title. Also include the type of action represented (e.g., final rule, proposed rule to amend, notice, etc.).

LEGISLATIVE SERVICES

"Statement of Organization, Functions, and Delegations of Authority (National Institutes of Health), Notice" (ID no. 428721; 57 lines;). Text from: *Federal Register Text* (On-line database). Referenced: 9/15/92, 9:23 a.m. EST. Available on: *LEGI-SLATE*, LEGI-SLATE, Inc., Washington; Internet address: legislate.com.

"Tribal Management Program for American Indians/Alaska Natives: Grants Application Announcement,

Notice" (57 FR 54986-01; 32 pages). Text from: *FR* (On-line database). Referenced: 11/24/92, 8:30 a.m. EST. Available on: *WESTLAW*, West Publishing Co., St. Paul, Minn.

ELECTRONIC BULLETIN BOARD

"Worker Protection Standard, Hazard Information, Hand Labor Tasks on Cut Flowers and Ferns Exception, Final Rule and Proposed Rules" (40 CFR Parts 156 and 170; 534802 bytes; 8/31/92). Text from: 5738102.TXT (Computer file). Referenced: 9/15/92, 1:25 p.m. EST. Available on: *The Federal Bulletin Board* (Electronic bulletin board). Government Printing Office, Washington; 202-512-1397.

E 8.5   Regulations

Most electronic forms of regulations are updated more frequently than the update cycle for the print version. For this reason it is very important to include a date indicating the last changes made to the electronic version. The source of this information will vary between electronic sources. The following examples show two different ways electronic sources provide this information.

CODE OF FEDERAL REGULATIONS (CFR)

"Minimum Wage Determinations (as changed July 15, 1991)" (Title 41 *Code of Federal Regulations*, Pts. 50-202; 19 lines). Text from: *Daily CFR* (On-line database). Referenced: 11/18/92, 3:03 p.m. EST. Available on: *LEGI-SLATE*, LEGI-SLATE, Inc., Washington; Internet address: legislate.com.

"Minimum Wage Determinations" (56 *Federal Register* 32258, July 15, 1991) (Title 41 *Code of Federal Regulations*, Pts. 50-202; 2 pages). Text from: *CFR* (On-line database). Referenced: 11/18/92, 3:30 p.m. EST. Available on: *WESTLAW*, West Publishing Co., St. Paul, Minn.

STATE REGULATIONS

"Physical Education and Athletics" (Title 22 *Pennsylvania Code*, Sec. 5.10; adopted Feb. 10, 1984; 5 pages).

> Text from: *PA-ADC* (On-line database). Referenced: 12/2/92, 5:50 p.m. EST. Available on: *WESTLAW*, West Publishing Co., St. Paul, Minn.

E 8.6   **Court Opinions**

A wide variety of court opinions are available in electronic sources. Include the following information for each decision before the elements described in E 7.1-7.2:

1) full name of the case (plaintiff v. defendant);
2) court (if not included in database or file name) and all identifying case citations, docket number or order numbers (these may be listed in some finding tools);
3) date of the decision; and
4) a parallel citation to the official or unofficial source (if provided).

U.S. SUPREME COURT

The Hermes project made U.S. Supreme Court decisions available quickly in a variety of locations.

> Pennsylvania v. Muniz, June 27, 1990 (MSG#124; Select menu options: The Courthouse/The Supreme Court Opinions (Project Hermes)) (Computer file). Referenced: 11/23/92, 10:10 p.m. CST. Available on: *Cleveland Freenet* (Electronic bulletin board); Internet address: 584@cleveland.freenet.edu.

STATE COURTS

> Commonwealth of Pennsylvania v. Warren Peterson, August 19, 1991 (408 *Pa. Super.* 22, 596 *A.2d* 172; 55 pages). Text from: *PA-CS* (On-line database). Referenced: 2/5/92, 3:35 p.m. EST. Available on: *WESTLAW*, West Publishing Co., St. Paul, Minn.

ADMINISTRATIVE COURTS

> Application of Midway Airlines, Inc. for an Emergency Exemption from Sections 408 and 409 of the Federal Aviation Act and Part 315 of the Board's Regulations (Civil Aeronautics Board; Order 84-9-37; Docket 42453; Sept. 13, 1984; 1984 CAB LEXIS 158). Text from: *Trans* (Library), *CAB* (File name) (On-line

database). Referenced: 11/13/91, 2:34 p.m. EST. Available on: *Lexis/Nexis*, Mead Data Central, Dayton, Ohio.

UNPUBLISHED DECISIONS WITHOUT A CASE NAME

1986 N.Y. City Tax LEXIS 68; FLR(109)-UT/GC-11/86 (New York City Department of Finance; Dec. 3, 1986). Text from: *Sttax* (Library), *NY* (File name) (On-line database). Referenced: 1/3/93, 10:12 a.m. EST. Available on: *Lexis/Nexis*, Mead Data Central, Dayton, Ohio.

ATTORNEY GENERAL OPINIONS

Formal Opinion No. 91-F9 (Office of the Attorney General of New York; Dec. 31, 1991; 1991 N.Y. AG LEXIS 88). Text from: *Insrlw* (Library), *NYAG* (File name) (On-line database). Referenced: 10/23/92, 4:05 p.m. EST. Available on: *Lexis/Nexis*, Mead Data Central, Dayton, Ohio.

NON-UNITED STATES COURTS

Mary Hanrahan, John Hanrahan and Selina Hanrahan v. Merck Sharp & Dohme (Ireland) Ltd. (The Supreme Court; 1982, no. 2138 P 1985 no. 316, transcript; 5 July 1988). Text from: *Irelnd* (Library), *Cases* (File name) (On-line database). Referenced: 12/2/92, 1:45 p.m. EST. Available on: *Lexis/Nexis*, Mead Data Central, Dayton, Ohio.

Eileen Garland v. British Rail Engineering Ltd. (Reference for a preliminary ruling from the House of Lords of the United Kingdom) (Case 12/81 (Opinion); Feb. 9, 1982; Doc. no: 681J0012). Text from: *Bas-Cen* (On-line database). Referenced: 6/8/92, 3:00 p.m. EST. Available on: *Celex*. Commission of the European Communities, Brussels. (Text available in most European Communities official languages).

E 8.7   Official Journal of the European Communities

The *Official Journal of the European Communities* includes directives, regulations, treaties, speeches, etc. Most systems have developed a unique identifier for each *Official Journal* entry. This identifier should be included in parentheses immediately following the entry title. When a unique identifier is not included, cite the print equivalent of the *Official Journal* and include the series number (C, L, Annex, Supplement). Cite the title in the language version you have used.

> "Proposal for a Council Directive Amending Directive 66/403/EEC on the Marketing of Seed Potatoes" (COM (90)134 final; Doc. no: 590PC0134). Text from: *Bas-Cen* (On-line database). Referenced: 2/5/92, 2:45 p.m. EST. Available on: *Celex*. Commission of the European Communities, Brussels. (Text available in most European Communities official languages).

E 8.8   Treaties

The full text of treaties will frequently be included in the text of databases containing the full text of sources.

> "Agreement between the European Economic Community and the Republic of Sierra Leone on Fishing off Sierra Leone" (Doc. no: 290A0515(01)). Text from: *Bas-Cen* (On-line database). Referenced: 2/5/92, 2:45 p.m. EST. Available on: *Celex*. Commission of the European Communities, Brussels. (Text available in most European Communities official languages).

> "Convention on Future Multilateral Cooperation in North-East Atlantic Fisheries" (Doc. no: 280A1118(01)). Text from: *CELEX-TRTY* (On-line database). Referenced: 1/2/93, 9:55 a.m. EST. Available on: *WESTLAW*, West Publishing Co., St. Paul, Minn.

E 8.9   Economic Report of the President

> *Economic Report of the President, 1991* (ID no. CE ERP; 204 records). Text from: U.S. Department of Commerce. Economics and Statistics Administration. *NESE DB: National Economic, Social and Environmental Data Bank* (CD-ROM). Experimental [edition]. Washington, Apr. 1992. (System requirements: IBM PC or compatible, at least 640KB memory,

DOS 3.1 or higher, *Microsoft Extensions* 2.0 or later, CD-ROM drive; includes access software: *Browse*; C1.88/2: Apr. 1992).

E 8.10   Census

A citation to U.S. census data in electronic format should include a complete title followed by the census year. Since some census data has been reissued, it is particularly important to include the issue date in the citation.

> U.S. Bureau of the Census. *Census of Agriculture: State Data File, County Data File (Including U.S. Totals), 1987* (CD-ROM). Washington, Aug. 1990. (dBase format; system requirements: IBM PC or compatible, CD-ROM drive; accompanied by: *Technical Documentation*; C3.277:Ag9/987).

> U.S. Bureau of the Census. *Census of Population and Housing: Summary Tape File 3A, 1990* (CD90-3A) (CD-ROM). Washington, Sept. 1992. (dBase format; system requirements: IBM PC or compatible, MS-DOS 3.0 or higher, *Microsoft Extensions* 2.0 or higher, 640KB RAM, CD-ROM drive, can be used with Apple Macintosh system; includes access software: *Browse*; C3.282/2:CD90-3).

E 8.10a   Parts

It is equally likely that you will need to cite a specific subset of census data. This may take several forms: a numbered volume within a set; a single CD-ROM within a set; a pre-defined table produced by access software provided with the electronic data; or a customized data subset compiled from a software package not provided with the electronic data. The following examples illustrate these variations.

A NUMBERED VOLUME WITHIN A SET

> U.S. Bureau of the Census. *Economic Censuses, 1987; Volume 1, Report Series* (CD-ROM). Release 1D. Washington, Nov. 1991. (3,500 files in dBase format; system requirements: IBM PC or compatible, CD-ROM drive; includes access software: *Profile1*,

Prodemo1, *Extract* (version 1.3); accompanied by: *Technical Documentation;* C3.277:Ec7/987/v.1/ Release 1D).

A SINGLE CD-ROM WITHIN A SET

U.S. Bureau of the Census. *Census of Population and Housing: Block Statistics, 1990: Middle-Atlantic Division (New Jersey, New York. Pennsylvania)* (CD90-1B-2) (CD-ROM). Reissued. Washington, Sept. 1992. (dBase format; system requirements: IBM PC or compatible, MS-DOS 3.0 or higher, *Microsoft Extensions* 2.0 or higher, 640KB RAM, CD-ROM drive, can be used with Apple Macintosh system; includes access software: *Browse*; C3.282:CD90-1B-2).

U.S. Bureau of the Census. *Tiger/Line Census Files, 1990: Florida (Pinellas-Washington), Idaho* (CD-ROM). Washington, July 1991. (System requirements: IBM PC or compatible, 640KB memory, *Microsoft Extensions* 2.0 or higher, can be used with Apple Macintosh system; accompanied by documentation on disk; C3.279:F66/2/990/CD).

A PRE-DEFINED TABLE

Some sources include a menu-driven interface that allows the user to define a specific data table. Include the following information when citing a specific table provided by the menu-driven interface from census data. To help the user locate more quickly the exact table you have used, include as much information about geography and summary levels as possible (this will also help avoid confusion with duplicate place names):

1) table name (e.g., "General profile," "Families");
2) Summary Level (Sumlvl) (e.g., 161, 040) and place names for each geography level (e.g., state, county, place).

"Detailed Race (040 Pennsylvania, 161 Columbia Borough)." Data from: U.S. Bureau of the Census. *Census of Population and Housing, Summary Tape File 1C, United States Summary, 1990* (CD90-1C) (CD-ROM). Washington, Feb. 1992. (dBase format; system requirements: IBM PC or compatible, 640KB memory, *Microsoft Extensions* 2.0 or higher, can be used with Apple Macintosh system; includes access software: *Browse*; C3.282:990-1C).

"Income, Education, Labor Force & Housing Characteristics (STF3): Centre County, Pennsylvania, Median Family Income in 1989." (Select menu options: 18.5.2.39.3.6, July 3, 1992). Data from: *CENDATA* (On-line database). Referenced: 12/15/92, 2:34 p.m. EST. Available on: *DIALOG*, Palo Alto, Cal.; Internet address: dialog.com.

"Households: Total 1990 (in Thousands): Pennsylvania." (Select menu options: States/Households/BTHOUS90 /AHOUS90S). Data from: *Demographic & Economic Database Files* (On-line database). Referenced: 11/18/92, 3:56 p.m. EST. Available on: *EDIN: Economic Development Information Network* (Electronic bulletin board). Pennsylvania State Data Center; Bitnet address: psuvm.

A DATA SUBSET COMPILED FROM CENSUS DATA

When a census data subset is created with a software package (*EXTRACT*, *dBase*, etc.) that allows the user to create customized data subsets, it is only necessary to indicate the source of the data (e.g., the volume number in the set) and the issue or release date. The phrase "compiled from:" indicates to the reader that the data can be found on the electronic source cited.

Compiled from: U.S. Bureau of the Census. *Census of Population and Housing, Summary Tape File 1A, 1990: Middle Atlantic Division (Vol. 2): New Jersey, Pennsylvania* (CD90-1A-2-2) (CD-ROM). Washington, 1992. (dBase format; system requirements: IBM PC or compatible, 640KB memory, *Microsoft Extensions* 2.0 or higher, can be used with Apple Macintosh system; accompanied by: *Technical Documentation*; C3.282:990/CD90-1A-2-2).

E 8.11   Statistical Abstract

Tables from the *Statistical Abstract* are available in a variety of electronic formats. Because it is an annual print publication, be sure to distinguish between the versions by including the edition number (if it is provided) or, in its absence, the year. Because the *Statistical Abstract* consists largely of statistical tables, it is more likely you will be citing a specific table than the entire volume.

> "Value of Privately Owned Nonresidential Building Projects" (ID Number: CN STATAB TAB1264). Data from: U.S. Bureau of the Census. *Statistical Abstract, 1992* (Computer file). Available on: U.S. Department of Commerce. Economics and Statistics Administration. *NESE DB: National Economic, Social and Environmental Data Bank* (CD-ROM). Experimental [edition]. Washington, Apr. 1992. (System requirements: IBM PC or compatible, at least 640KB memory, DOS 3.1 or higher, *Microsoft Extensions* 2.0 or later, CD-ROM drive; includes access software: *Browse*; C1.88/2: Apr. 1992).

E 8.12   **Government Statistics with a Software Interface Created by a Commercial Vendor**

Since government information cannot be copyrighted, many companies are now packaging government information with a software interface. This combination allows the user to create maps or other graphic images or to perform statistical analysis. In these cases, the only indication that you are using government information may be a list of data sources included somewhere in the electronic source's user manual or technical documentation. Frequently the list of sources also reveals that the commercial vendor has combined a variety of government statistics onto a single electronic source (e.g., data from the *Census of Agriculture, Census of Population and Housing*, and *County Business Patterns*, combined into one data set).

Further complicating this scenerio, the software interface provided by the commercial vendor may allow the creation of a unique image, map, or data table with this data without also allowing the adequate identification of the specific data source used to create it. In these situations you should cite the title of the entire source. The variety of combinations possible will also require you to be alert to include information about the data source if it is separate from the software interface (e.g., a CD-ROM containing the data and the software on a floppy disk—the CD-ROM having its own title and the software also having its own name or title).

DATA AND SOFTWARE IN SAME FORMAT

> Compiled from: *PC Globe* (Floppy disk includes data and software). Version 3.0. Tempe, Ariz.: PC Globe, 1989. (System requirements: IBM PC or compatible with 512KB RAM, one or two floppy drives or 1 floppy drive and a hard disk, DOS 2.0 or later, IBM graphics adapter; accompanied by: *User's Guide*).

DATA AND SOFTWARE IN DIFFERENT FORMATS

> Compiled from: *Supermap* (Software on floppy disk) and *U.S. Bureau of the Census, 1980 Census: Disc 1, Data* (CD-ROM). Melbourne, Australia: Space-Time Research, 1988. (System requirements: IBM PC or compatible with at least 4MB free space, IBM compatible enhanced graphics adapter (EGA) with 256KB graphics memory, CD-ROM drive, *Microsoft Extensions*; accompanied by: *Supermap User's Guide and Reference*; distributed by Chadwyck-Healy, Alexandria, Va.).

PARTS

Some commercial sources will allow you to produce statistical tables from data and are structured to allow the user to know the file name they have used. In these cases, the actual file can be cited as an electronic part.

> "Percent Persons 35 to 44 Years" (Coverage: POP88S; file name: P_35_44). Data from: *ArcUSA 1:2M (Coterminous U.S.)* (CD-ROM). Edition 1. Redlands, Cal.: Environmental Systems Research Institute, Oct. 1, 1992. (dBase format; system requirements: *Arc-View* for *Windows*, CD-ROM reader; accompanied by: *User's Guide & Data Reference*).

However, when data from more than one data file are used, it is only necessary to use the phrase "Compiled from:" and the electronic source.

Compiled from: *ArcUSA 1:2M (Coterminous U.S.)* (CD-ROM). Edition 1. Redlands, Cal.: Environmental Systems Research Institute, Oct. 1, 1992. (dBase format; system requirements: CD-ROM reader; accompanied by: *User's Guide & Data Reference*).

E 8.13   Patents and Trademarks

The full text of patents (or parts of patents) including the drawings and trademark images are becoming more readily available in electronic format. Preceding the information included in E 1-7.2, a patent image citation should also include:

1) the patent title;
2) the name of the patentee;
3) a unique identifying number (e.g., the patent number); and
4) the date the patent was issued.

"Device for Supporting Bound Material" by Robert D. Rose. U.S. Patent 4,793,633 (Dec. 27, 1988). Available on: U.S. Patent and Trademark Office. Office of Patent Depository Library. *Patent Image-Full Text* (CD-ROM). Test Disc 1, weekly issue Dec. 27, 1988. n.p., n.d. (includes access software: *CD-Answer Retrieval Software*).

For trademark images the following information should be included in parentheses after the title of the trademark:

1) status (registered, pending, etc.) and date;
2) date published;
3) owner, preceded by "owner:"; and
4) unique identifying number, such as the serial number, database accession number, etc.

"PennState 1855" (Registered, Nov. 17, 1992; serial number 74-081-576; August 25, 1992; owner: Pennsylvania State University; *DIALOG* accession number 04881576). Referenced: 12/10/92, 6:54 p.m. EST. Text and image from: *Trademarkscan-Federal* (File 226) (On-line database). Available on: *DIALOG*. Palo Alto, Cal.; Internet address, dialog.com. (System requirements to view image: *DIALOGLINK* (software) 1.2 or later for IBM PC or compatible or *Imagecatcher* (software) for Apple Macintosh).

E 8.14   Securities and Exchange Commission (SEC) Reports

Several electronic sources provide information (extracts) taken from reports (10-K, 10-Qs, 8-Ks, etc.) filed with the SEC. Unlike the microformat of these publications, these sources are not the full text of these reports, but rather a reformatted version that may also incorporate information from additional non-government sources. Because the exact SEC form number does not correspond to each of these records, these records should be identified as a generic "company report" in parentheses following the company name. The date the database or the CD-ROM was referenced is extremely important in these citations because these records are updated on a regular basis using newly released SEC reports.

In addition to the information described in E 1-7, a citation to these reports should begin with:

1) the company name; and
2) any unique record identifier (stock symbol, record number, etc.).

> Merck & Co. (Record no. M419100000; company report). Available on: *Compact Disclosure* (CD-ROM). Nov. 1992. (System requirements: IBM PC or compatible, at least 512KB memory and 1.25 MB free on hard disk, DOS 3.3 or higher; CD-ROM drive; accompanied by: *User's Manual*).

> Merck & Co. (MRK; company report). Text from: *Disclosure Database* (On-line database). Referenced: 12/1/92, 12:30 p.m. CST. Available on: *Dow Jones News/Retrieval*, Princeton, N.J.

E 8.15   Computer Tapes

A wide variety of second-party sources (such as ICPSR) make government information available on computer tape. Some second-party sources may make changes to the original government data; thus, a citation to these computer tapes must include the source of the tape, as well as the agency or persons collecting the data. In addition to the information described in E 1-6, include the word "Distributor" in parentheses following the name of a second party source for a computer tape containing government information.

> U.S. Department of Education. National Center for Education Statistics. *High School and Beyond, 1980: A Longitudinal Survey of Students in the United States* (ICPSR 7896) (Computer tape). Ann Arbor, Mich.: Inter-University Consortium for Political and Social Research (Distributor), n.d.

> Rabier, Jacques-Rene. *Euro-Barometer 25: Holiday Travel and Environmental Problems, Apr. 1986* (ICPSR 8616) (Computer tape). First ICPSR Edition. Ann Arbor, Mich.: Inter-University Consortium for Political and Social Research (Distributor), 1988.

> U.S. Bureau of the Census. *Census of Population and Housing: Summary Tape Files 1A*, 1990 (ICPSR 9575) (Computer tape). First ICPSR Release. Ann Arbor, Mich.: Inter-University Consortium for Political and Social Research (Distributor), June 1991.

E 8.16   Software

Government agencies can be the source of a great deal of highly specialized software. Software citations will usually include personal authors and may also reflect joint projects between more than one agency or department. In addition to the information described in E 1-6, include the version number as an edition statement (see Fig. 21).

> U.S. Centers for Disease Control. *EPI Info: A Word Processing, Database, and Statistics System for Epidemiology on Microcomputers* by Andrew G. Dean et al. (Software). Version 5.01. Atlanta, Ga., 1990. (Compressed format; system requirements: IBM compatible, PC- or MS-DOS 2.0 or higher, 512KB RAM, at least one floppy disk drive, a

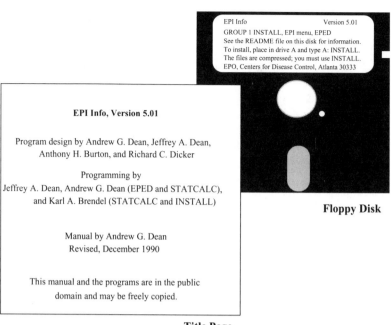

EPI Info   Version 5.01
GROUP 1 INSTALL, EPI menu, EPED
See the README file on this disk for information.
To install, place in drive A and type A: INSTALL.
The files are compressed; you must use INSTALL.
EPO, Centers for Disease Control, Atlanta 30333

EPI Info, Version 5.01

Program design by Andrew G. Dean, Jeffrey A. Dean,
Anthony H. Burton, and Richard C. Dicker

Programming by
Jeffrey A. Dean, Andrew G. Dean (EPED and STATCALC),
and Karl A. Brendel (STATCALC and INSTALL)

Floppy Disk

Manual by Andrew G. Dean
Revised, December 1990

This manual and the programs are in the public
domain and may be freely copied.

Title Page

Figure 21: Title Page from User's Manual/Software on Floppy Disk

graphics adapter board to produce graphs; accompanied by: *Manual*, 384 pp.; HE20.7002:Ep 4.8).

U.S. Environmental Protection Agency. *Hyperventilate: A Software Guidance System Created for Vapor Extraction Applications* by Paul C. Johnson (EPA 500-C-B-92-001) (Software). Version 1.01. Washington: Government Printing Office, 1992. (Solid Waste and Emergency Response [OS-420-WF]). (System requirements: Apple Macintosh with 1MB RAM, Apple *Hypercard* sofware program 2.0 or greater; accompanied by: *Hyperventilate Users Manual*; EP1.8:H99).

E 8.17   E-mail Messages

Many of the government EBBs also offer the user the ability to send and receive electronic mail messages. Include the following information:

1) Name of the person the message is from, including e-mail address, if available;
2) subject or title of the message followed by format qualifier;
3) name of the person, EBB, or discussion group, to whom the message was sent, preceded by "message to:" and followed in parentheses by the electronic address, if available;
4) original date of the message;
5) length of message, if provided by the system; and
6) name of EBB or discussion group containing the message (if appropriate).

PERSONAL E-MAIL MESSAGE

Cheney, Debora (DLC@PSULIAS). Subject: *Citing Electronic Formats* (Electronic mail). Message to: Elizabeth Montgomery (EBM@HARVARDA), Dec. 5, 1992.

MESSAGE TO A LISTSERV

Davis, J. Mike. Subject: *Chronic Disease Prevention CD-ROM* (Electronic mail). Message to: GOVDOC-L Discussion List (GOVDOC-L@PSUVM.Bitnet), Mar. 2, 1992.

Style Manuals

Brightbill, George D., and Wayne C. Maxson. *Citation Manual for United States Government Publications*. Philadelphia: Center for the Study of Federalism, Temple University, 1974.

Campbell, William Giles, and Stephen Vaughn Ballou. *Form and Style: Theses, Reports, Term Papers*. Boston: Houghton Mifflin, 1990.

Clark, Suzanne M. *Cartographic Citations, A Style Guide*. Chicago: American Library Association, 1992.

Fleischer, Eugene B. *A Style Manual for Citing Microform and Nonprint Media*. Chicago: American Library Association, 1978.

A Manual of Style. 14th ed. rev. Chicago: University of Chicago Press, 1986.

Modern Language Association. *MLA Handbook for Writers of Research Papers, Theses, and Dissertations*. New York: MLA, 1984.

Roistacha, Richard C. *A Style Manual for Machine-Readable Data Files and Their Documentation*. Washington: Government Printing Office, 1980.

Rothman, Marie H. *Citation Rules and Forms for United Nations Documents and Publications*. Brooklyn, NY: Long Island University Press, 1971.

Turabian, Kate L. *A Manual for Writers of Term Papers, Theses and Dissertations*. 5th ed. Chicago: University of Chicago Press, 1987.

U.N. Dag Hammarskjold Library. *Bibliographical Style Manual* (ST/LIB/SER.B/8). New York, 1963.

A Uniform System of Citation. 14th ed. Cambridge, Mass.: Harvard Law Review Association, 1986.

U.S. Department of Justice. *A Style Manual for Machine-Readable Data Files and Their Documentation*. Washington: Government Printing Office, 1980. (J29.9:SD-T-3).

U.S. Department of Justice. Tax Division. *Citation and Style Manual*. Washington, 1988. (J1.8/2:C49/3).

U.S. Library of Congress. Reference Department. General Reference and Bibliography Division. *Bibliographical Procedures & Style* by Blanche Prichard McCrum and Helen Dudenbostel Jones. Washington: Government Printing Office, 1966.

U.S. National Archives and Records Administration. *Citing Records in the National Archives of the United States*. Washington, 1986. (AE1.113:17).

Van Leunen, Mary-Claire. *A Handbook for Scholars*. Rev. ed. New York: Oxford University Press, 1992.

Standard Reference Sources for Government Information

United States

American Foreign Policy Index. Bethesda, Md.: Congressional Information Service, Inc.

American Statistics Index (ASI). Bethesda, Md.: Congressional Information Service, Inc.

Andriot, John. *Guide to U.S. Government Publications.* McLean, Va.: Documents Index.

CIS/Index to Congressional Publications. Bethesda, Md.: Congressional Information Service, Inc.

CIS U.S. Congressional Committee Hearings Index. Bethesda, Md.: Congressional Information Service, Inc.

CIS U.S. Congressional Committee Prints Index. Bethesda, Md.: Congressional Information Service, Inc.

CIS U.S. Serial Set Index. Bethesda, Md.: Congressional Information Service, Inc.

Congressional Index. Chicago: Commerce Clearing House.

Congressional Masterfile (CD-ROM). Bethesda, Md.: Congressional Information Service, Inc.

Foreign Broadcast Information Service Electronic Index (CD-ROM). New Canaan, Conn.: Newsbank/Readex.

Index to U.S. Government Periodicals. Chicago: Infordata International, Inc.

LEGI-SLATE (on-line database). Washington: LEGI-SLATE, Inc.

Resources in Education. Phoenix, Ariz.: Oryx Press.

U.S. Bureau of the Census. *Census Catalog.* Washington: Government Printing Office.

U.S. Government Printing Office. *List of Classes of United States Government Publications Available for Selection by Depository Libraries.* Washington: Government Printing Office.

_____. *Monthly Catalog of U.S. Government Publications.* Washington: Government Printing Office.

U.S. National Technical Information Service (NTIS). *Government Reports Announcements and Index.* Springfield, Va.: NTIS.

United States Government Manual. Washington: Government Printing Office.

State, Local, Regional

Index to Current Urban Documents. Westport, Conn.: Greenwood Press.

State Bluebooks and Reference Publications: A Selected Bibliography. Lexington, Ky.: Council of State Governments, 1983.

Statistical Masterfile, ASI, SRI and IIS on CD-ROM. Bethesda, Md.: Congressional Information Service, Inc.

Statistical Reference Index (SRI). Bethesda, Md.: Congressional Information Service, Inc.

U.S. Library of Congress. *Monthly Checklist of State Publications.* Washington: Library of Congress.

International

Documents Oficiales de la Organización de los Estados Americanos. Washington: Organization of American States.

FAO Documentation. Rome: Food and Agriculture Organization of the United Nations.

Index to International Statistics (IIS). Bethesda, Md.: Congressional Information Service, Inc.

Index to the United Nations Documents and Publications (CD-ROM). New Canaan, Conn.: Newsbank/Readex.

International Bibliography. New York: Unipub.

UNDOC. New York: United Nations.

UNESCO List of Documents and Publications. Paris: UNESCO.

Yearbook of International Organizations. Brussels: Union of International Associations.

Foreign

Most countries have a listing of their publications. For the most complete and current list of these catalogs consult:

Westfall, Gloria, ed. *Guide to Official Publications of Foreign Countries.* Bethesda, Md.: Congressional Information Service, Inc., 1990.

GLOSSARY

A

Act: a piece of legislation that has been approved by one chamber of the U.S. Congress. An Act becomes a Public Law after it has gone through the legislative process and is signed by the President. (Note: in some states laws are called Acts.)

Agency Report Numbers: unique numbers assigned to published documents. These numbers are alphanumerical and are usually located in the upper or lower corners of the cover and/or title page (see Fig. 7).

Agricultural Experiment Station/Agricultural Extension Service: agencies established by the U.S. Department of Agriculture, in cooperation with states, counties, and universities, to serve agricultural and rural communities.

ANSI (American National Standards Institute): an organization which attempts to set industry and engineering standards for various products. One group within ANSI deals with bibliographic standards.

B

Bibliographic Data Sheet: a form on the front or back of technical reports, but also found in other document types. The standard sheet contains information on authors, title, date, sponsoring and performing agencies, contract number, report number, subject headings, and abstract.

Bill: the most common form by which legislation is introduced in the U.S. Congress and state legislatures. In Congress all bill numbers are prefixed by H.R. or S. for House of Representatives or Senate, respectively.

C

Cataloging: the process by which a library describes the physical makeup and intellectual contents of a book.

CD-ROM (Compact Disc-Read Only Memory): a 4 3/4" disk that is used to store large volumes of text, numbers, or images. Requires a special reader attached to a personal computer.

CIP (Cataloging in Publication): initial cataloging provided by the publisher when a book is printed. This information is usually located on the back of the title page and frequently is labeled "CIP."

Clearinghouses: organizations established primarily to provide copies of reports to individuals and groups.

COM-Docs: a class of documents submitted by the European Communities Commission to the Council of Ministers. These may be reports, proposals for action, etc. They were not indexed and were difficult to obtain until 1983 when the EC began to issue them on microfiche with an index.

Committee Prints: written for Congressional committees, these publications provide background information on a piece of legislation or on a specific topic.

Computer Tape: computer-readable magnetic tape used for information storage.

Conference Committee: a committee, composed of House and Senate members, which attempts to eliminate disagreements between Congressional chambers by reaching a compromise on a piece of legislation.

Conference Report: a report issued by a conference committee.

Contract Number: a series of numbers assigned to publications contracted for a government. These numbers are usually alphanumeric but are not necessarily unique to a document. Therefore, they are not considered valid citation elements.

Cooperative Publications: documents which are jointly written and funded by more than one governmental or intergovernmental entity.

D

Documents, Congressional: publications produced by the U.S. Congress covering a variety of materials, such as reports of committee activities, communications to Congress from the President and other executive agencies, miscellaneous items from patriotic groups, annual reports to Congress, and reports from individual legislative fact-finding missions.

E

Electronic Bulletin Board (EBB): a computer system accessible via a modem that can serve as an information and message system.

Electronic Mail: a message transmitted between sender and receiver via a communications network.

Ellipses: a form of punctuation (. . .) which indicates the omission of information. In citations, ellipses are usually employed when shortening title data.

ERIC (Educational Resources Information Center): a national information network of 16 clearinghouses managed by the Office of Educational Research and Improvement. Publications available from ERIC are identified by an agency report number beginning with ED.

European Communities: an economic, social, and, sometimes, political union of Western European countries (France, Belgium, Denmark, Germany, Greece, Ireland, Italy, Luxembourg, the Netherlands, the United Kingdom, Spain, and Portugal).

Extract: A software program developed by the U.S. Bureau of the Census to be used to select and "extract" data subsets from CD-ROMs released by the Bureau of the Census. This data, once extracted, can be used with another software package, such as *dBase* or *LOTUS 1-2-3*, for analysis and creating graphic images.

F

FBIS: see JPRS and FBIS.

Floppy Disk: a storage medium for computer files and software. May be either 3 1/2 or 5 1/4-inch.

Frame: an individual page in a microform. In microfiche the location of the frame is occasionally designated by an alphanumeric code (e.g., C5).

FTP (File Transfer Protocol) Site: the location of a machine-readable file that can be transferred from one computer to another over a network such as the Internet.

G

Gopher Server: a network address that includes access to a Gopher program.

GPO (Government Printing Office): the printer to Congress and the major federal printer/distributor. The GPO is the agency responsible for the federal depository system, maintaining the SuDoc system, and issuing the *Monthly Catalog of U.S. Government Publications.*

Grant Number: see Contract Number.

H

Hearing: a meeting (usually public) held by a Congressional committee to investigate a bill, to provide legislative oversight, or to gather background information on a particular issue. Also, the written testimony and discussion from such a meeting.

HMSO (Her Majesty's Stationery Office): The official printing agency for Great Britain.

I

ICPSR (Inter-university Consortium for Political and Social Research): a consortium, located at the University of Michigan, that provides to its members (largely academic libraries) computer tapes of data collected for or useful for political or social science research.

IGO (Intergovernmental Organization): an international organization whose members are countries, rather than individuals or institutions.

Imprint: a bibliographic term for the facts of publication—place of publication, publisher, and date of publication or copyright.

Internet: an international network that connects similar smaller networks creating a national electronic highway that allows the user to access a wide variety of databases, FTP sites, and e-mail addresses.

ISBN (International Standard Book Number): a unique multi-digit number which publishers assign to books. It is frequently used as an ordering and verification number by booksellers.

Item Numbers: numbers used by depository libraries to select federal publications. These numbers appear in the *Monthly Catalog of U.S. Government Publications,* preceded by the depository black dot. Since there is not necessarily a direct title to item number correspondence, these numbers are not included as citation elements.

J

JPRS (Joint Publications Research Service) and FBIS (Foreign Broadcast Information Service): translating agencies of the Central Intelligence Agency that monitor print and broadcast media worldwide.

L

Loose-leafs: publications issued in a notebook format, which allows for easy updating. Frequently, pages are dated either at the top or at the bottom.

M

Masthead: the banner at the top of a publication which contains the basic bibliographic information needed to complete a citation (e.g., title, volume numbers, etc.) commonly found on a title page.

Mimeographed document: a document produced internally, often identifiable by its typeface.

Mimeo (U.N.): preliminary records of the U.N. General Assembly, Economic and Social Council, Security Council, and the Trusteeship Council. Many of them are later reissued as U.N. official records. They are identified by a series/ symbol number and by the lack of a sales number or an official record designation.

N

National Technical Information Service (NTIS): a clearinghouse established within the U.S. Department of Commerce to distribute all forms of scientific, technical, and government-contracted reports.

O

Official Gazette: a periodical publication issued by a foreign government that is used to inform the public of government actions such as new laws and regulations.

On-line Database: a machine-readable computer file, containing text, data, or images, that can be reached via a telecommunications connection.

On-line Database Vendor: a commercial company that provides telecommunications access to computer files. Users may search these computer files for a fee.

Ordinances: laws of a municipality, passed by a municipal council or its equivalent. Such laws usually govern zoning, safety, building, noise, etc.

P

Parliamentary Body: used here to designate international groups which meet, debate, and pass resolutions, but which do not have legislative power (e.g., the U.N. General Assembly; Council of Europe Parliamentary Assembly; European Parliament).

Parliamentary Papers: a collection of governmental reports from executive and parliamentary agencies, which are gathered together and republished under the auspices of the parliament. They generally appear as a numbered series.

Periodical: a title published at specified intervals (e.g., weekly, monthly).

Printer's Number: a number assigned by a printer when publishing documents. The number may be item specific or may be assigned to a number of documents printed on a particular day. Therefore, it is not usually considered a valid citation element.

Project Hermes: a pilot project, coordinated by the U.S. federal government to provide machine-readable text of U.S. Supreme Court decisions to courts, the legal profession, libraries, and the press, so decisions can be disseminated more quickly and effectively.

Public Law: the official name of a piece of legislation passed by the U.S. government. Each Public Law has a P.L. number designating the Congress and chronological order of passage (e.g., PL 97-235).

Publication: material reproduced and distributed through formal means. This term is also used by some international organizations for works created especially for public sale (as opposed to documents or working papers). These works look like commercial press books and are treated as such by some libraries.

R

Readex Microprints: collections of government documents done by the Readex Corporation. Until 1982 the medium was micro-opaque cards; now they are on microfiche. UN Readex is filed by series/number; US Readex is filed by *Monthly Catalog* entry number.

Readme: a computer file frequently found on CD-ROMs, floppy disks, or EBBs that typically contains useful or necessary information, such as installation instructions, and that may not be available in print documentation or other sources.

Regulations: laws promulgated by executive agencies. They usually deal with the details of administering laws of legislative bodies.

Reports, Congressional: publications from a Congressional committee which recommend certain action, usually relating to a piece of legislation. Congressional reports present the committee's view of the legislative intent of a law.

Reprint: the republication of a document with no physical changes. Frequently, both the original and reprinting dates are listed on the document.

Resolution: a form of legislation in the U.S. Congress. Simple resolutions are designated by H.Res. or S.Res.; concurrent resolutions by H.Con.Res. or S.Con.Res.; joint resolutions by H.J.Res. or S.J.Res.

S

Sales Catalogs: for some international organizations, these are the only listings of the publications of the organization. They may contain indexes—by subject, title, author—and/or they may be organized broadly by subject. They are usually available free from the agency or from its sales agent.

Serial Set: the official compilation of Congressional reports and documents. Each volume in the set is numbered on the spine of the volume. The set began in 1817.

Series/Symbol Number: a number assigned to a document by the UN. It indicates the issuing body, the type of document, and its place in the series.

Slip Law: the first official publication of a U.S. statute, issued as an unbound pamphlet. Slip laws give the text of a law, references to other statutes amended by the law, and a brief history of the bill's passage into law.

Software: a machine-readable program that allows a user to manipulate, use, view, or analyze text, data, or images also in a machine-readable format.

Star Print: a reprint of a piece of legislation, ordered because of typographical errors in the original publication. It is designated by a star in the lower left corner of the bill.

State Data Centers: institutions sponsored in cooperation with the U.S. Bureau of the Census and state governments. The objective of these centers is to provide census data more efficiently to groups, businesses, and individuals.

Stock Number: a twelve-digit number used by the GPO for ordering purposes. Because stock numbers have only recently appeared in indexes and have not been assigned to all GPO documents, they are usually not included in a citation.

Superintendent of Documents (SuDoc) System: an alphanumeric numbering system used by most federal depository libraries to classify federal documents. The system is arranged hierarchically by issuing agency.

T

Technical Report Documentation Page: see Bibliographic Data Sheet.

Title Page: usually the first printed page in a book or document. Information found on the front of a title page includes author, publisher, and title. The back of a title page contains the date and place of publications. With some documents the title page and cover may be the same.

U

U.N. Official Records: final records of the sessions of the U.N. There are generally three types of official records: meetings record (verbatim or summary); supplements (reports, background material, etc.); and annexes (usually administrative information). Some official records do not fall into any of these classes.

University Press Books: books published by universities. Occasionally, university presses produce documents for the government.

Numbers refer to pages within Chapter 1. Alphanumerics refer to specific section of Chapters 2-6. Italicized alphanumerics index only to specific examples of a bibliographic citation problem with no textual explanations.

A

Abbreviation
  document types, Congressional, 12; *US 2.8*
  et al., US 2.6a; SLR 2.6a; I 2.6a; F 2.6b; E 2.6
  Latin, 11
  months, 12
  n.d., US 4.3b; SLR 4.3b; I 4.3b; F4.3c; E 4.3b
  n.p., US 4.1b; I 4.1a; F 4.1a; E 4.2b
  states, 12; SLR 1.1
Act, US 1.3f; US 8.13-13d; SLR 8.2
  defined, see Glossary
Agency report numbers, US 2.8; SLR 2.8; I 2.8; Table 3; F 6.1a; E 2.7
  Census, US 8.22c
  defined, see Glossary
  in series, US 5.1a
Agricultural experiment station, SLR 8.9-8.9a
  defined, see Glossary
Agricultural extension service, SLR 8.9-8.9a
  defined, see Glossary
American State Papers, US 8.15
Annals of Congress, US 8.9
ANSI, 3
  defined, see Glossary
Archives, US 8.31
  Freedom of Information Act material, US 8.32; SLR 8.12
  see also Clearinghouses
Article, US 7; SLR 7; I 7; F 7; E 7
  in document, US 7.2; SLR 7.2; I 7.2; F 7.2; E 7.4
  in encyclopedia, I 7.2
  in hearing, US 7.2
  in periodical, US 7.1-7.1c; US 8.25-8.26; SLR 7.1-7.1b; I 7.1; F.7.1; E 7.3
  in yearbook, I 7.2
ASI microfiche, *US 8.30a*
Audiovisual material, US 2.9; SLR 2.9; I 2.9

P

Pamphlet, US 6.2; SLR 6.2
Parliament (Canada), *F 1.5*; F 8.10
Parliament (U.K.), F 8.2a-8.2b; F 8.9
Parliamentary body
    defined, see Glossary
Parliamentary papers
    defined, see Glossary
Part
    book chapter, US 7.2; SLR 7.2; I 7.2; F 7.2; E 7.4
    debate, US 8.8a; I 8.9f; I 8.14
    encyclopedia article, US 7.2; I 7.2
    Foreign Relations of the U.S., US 8.16a
    insert in hearing, US 7.2
    journal entry, US 8.10-8.11
    loose-leaf, US 7.3; SLR 7.3; I 7.3
    paper in proceedings, US 7.2; I 7.2;
    press release, E 7.4
    speech, US 8.8-8.9; *US 8.19*; I 7.2; I 8.9d-8.9f; E 7.4
    statistical data, US 8.23a; SLR 8.6a; F 7.2; E 7.4
Patents, US 8.24; E 8.13
Periodical
    author, US 7.1-7.1b; SLR 7.1-7.1a; I 7.1; F 7.1; E 7.3
    defined, see Glossary
    issuing agency, US 7.1a; SLR 7.1; I 7.1; F 7.1
    no author, US 7.1c; SLR 7.1b; I 7.1; F 7.1
Place of publication, US 4.1-4.1b; SLR 4.1-4.1b; I 4.1-4.1a; F 4.1; E 4.1
    no place (n.p.), US 4.1b; I 4.1a; F 4.1a; E 4.1a
    where to find, US 4.1-4.1a; SLR 4.1; F 4; E 4.1
Poster, US 6.2; F 6.2
Press release, US 6.2; F 6.2; F 8.12; E 7.4
Printer's number, SLR 8.5b
    defined, see Glossary
Presidential news conference, *US 8.18a*
Presidential papers
    see *Public Papers of the Presidents; Weekly Compilation of Presidential Documents*
Proceedings
    see Conference proceedings
Proclamation (U.S. President), US 8.5; US 8.18
Project Hermes, *E 8.6*
    defined, see Glossary
Public law, US 8.3-8.4
    defined, see Glossary
Public Papers of the Presidents, US 8.19
Publication
    defined, see Glossary

U

Underlining, 11

UNESCO, *I 1; I 1.1b; I 1.5b; I 2.9; I 4.3;* I 8.5

    UNESCO Press, I 4.2b

United Nations

    conference, I 8.4

    Economic and Social Council, *I 1.1a; I 4.3c*

    film, I 2.9; I 6.2c

    General Assembly, *I 1.5a;* I 2.7; *I 2.9; I 6.1d*

    map, I 2.9

    mimeo, *I 1.1a;* I 2.7; I 4.3c; I 6.1c; Fig. 14

        defined, see Glossary

    Official Record, *I 1.5a;* I 3.1b; I 8.2-8.2e

        defined, see Glossary

    periodical, I 7.1

    Readex microprint, I 2.9; I 8.3d

    resolution, I 8.3-8.3d

    Security Council, *I 6.1d*

    series, I 5.1-5.1a

    series/symbol number, I 2.7; I 4.3c; I 7.1; I 8.2a-8.2b; I 8.2d-8.2e; I 8.3a-8.3b;

        I 8.3d

    treaties, I 8.6

    yearbook, I 7.2; I 8.5

United States Code, US 8.4-8.4a; E 8.3

United States Government Manual, US 8.2

United States Reports, US 8.7

United States Treaties, US 8.17

University press book, US 8.29; SLR 8.8a; I 4.2c

    defined, see Glossary

University publication

    as state document, SLR 8.8

    of agricultural extension service, SLR 8.9a

Unpublished material

    Freedom of Information Act, US 8.32; SLR 8.12

    mimeo, US 6.1; SLR 6.1; I 6.1c

Urban Documents Microfiche Collection, SLR 8.10

V

Video cassette, US 2.9; F 6.2

Volume number of periodical, US 7.1; SLR 7.1; I 7.1

W

Weekly Compilation of Presidential Documents, US 8.18-8.18a

Western European Union, I 8.16

WESTLAW databases, *E 8.1, E 8.3-8.6; E 8.8*

Workshops

    see Conference proceedings